GOD OUR FAT

Dr. A. K. Waters,
21, Moorland Drive,
Leeds 17,
West Yorkshire.

DOCTRINE AND DEVOTION I:

GOD OUR FATHER

Alan Sell

THE SAINT ANDREW PRESS
EDINBURGH

First published in 1980 by
THE SAINT ANDREW PRESS
121 George Street, Edinburgh EH2 4YN

Copyright © Alan Sell, 1980

ISBN 0 7152 0442 4

Printed in Great Britain by
Thomson Litho Ltd, East Kilbride, Scotland

Contents

PREFACE

In this series of books I seek to marry the spirit of enquiry with that of devotion. I have written with *audiences* of ministers, church members, and enquirers in mind and, although I have tried not to shirk difficult questions, my main emphasis has been affirmatory rather than argumentative. I have sought to ground upon the Bible, and I have drawn liberally on the testimony of the ages.

The plan of the series is simple. In Volume One I deal with the Christian doctrine of God; subsequent volumes will cover other major doctrines in turn. I begin with God as known in Christ, and the series will conclude with some reflections upon the Holy Trinity. I realise that the Trinity might have been expected to appear in Volume One, and I do believe that the triune God is the presupposition of Christian *theology*. But when we come to our ordinary Christian experience it seems to me that generally the case is otherwise: we begin with God-in-Christ, and affirmations about the Trinity are among the last we feel ready to make. At all events, the Trinity will be my culminating theme.

I give biblical references as they occur, but in order not to violate the eye with a surfeit of brackets and explanatory clauses, I append an index of persons in which each is accorded his birth and death dates (where known), together with a descriptive sentence. Readers possessed of the slightest powers of detection will swiftly tumble to the fact that the chapter titles are phrases from hymns quoted. Each chapter ends with suggested devotional material.

I am grateful to those members of United Reformed churches in Walsall with whom I worked through the material in this first volume; and I dedicate the entire venture to the congregations at Failsworth, Sedbergh, Dent, Worcester, Hallow and Ombersley, amongst whom I made mistakes and, I trust, learned something of the craft of ministering.

Alan P. F. Sell
West Midlands College of Higher Education,
Walsall.

1

The Brightest Image of His Grace

Christians know God. That is a mighty claim indeed, and many would say that we are deluding ourselves in making it. Others think that if not impossible, the affirmation of God is unnecessary. The French mathematician and astronomer Laplace, for example, is famed for having declared that he had no need of the God hypothesis; as far as he was concerned the idea of God was redundant. Undeterred, we persist in affirming God, and in claiming to know him. Why? Because he has made himself known to us and it would be dishonest or irrational to deny it. We could not know him unless he wished to be known; the initiative is always with him. But he *has* made himself known, and that supremely in Christ. In majestic Greek, of which our English translations are but an insipid reflection, the writer to the Hebrews avers: 'When in former times God spoke to our forefathers, he spoke in fragmentary and varied fashion through the prophets. But in this the final age he has spoken to us in the Son . . .' (Heb. 1: 1,2). Two very important points are made here:

(a) The writer not only declares that God speaks; he makes clear the *kind* of God who speaks. He is the one God who has made himself known supremely in Christ. The *one* God—we are not polytheists; made known supremely in Christ—we are not Jews or Muslims. Our God is God-in-Christ, and in his Son he has spoken as nowhere else. When God speaks, not only is information conveyed, but things happen. Jesus is the *Logos*, the Word of God, and that rich concept contains within it the ideas

1

of speech, thought and action. We believe that nowhere was God more decisively active, audible and visible than in the Cross-Resurrection event. So it is that when the fourth Gospel informs us that this 'Word [whilst in no way foregoing his divinity] became flesh; he came to dwell among us' (Jn. 1: 14)— to 'tabernacle' in our midst in a much more dramatic way than God of old had dwelt with Isreal (Exod. 25: 8; II Sam. 7: 6)— Jew and Greek alike are repelled. The Jews, recalling the text, 'A hanged man is offensive [or accursed] in the sight of God' (Deut. 21: 23), could not come to terms with the idea of a crucified Messiah; and the Greeks, because of their belief that matter is evil, found the idea of an enfleshed God 'a folly' (I Cor. 1: 23). Yet Christians claim that despite their unworthiness—indeed, in an important sense, *because* of their sin, God in Christ came and ever comes. He came 'not as a wayfaring man that tarries but for a night, but he *dwelt* among us' (Matthew Henry). So although 'No one has ever seen God (*cf.* Exod. 33: 20-23) . . . God's only Son, he who is nearest to the Father's heart, he has made him known' (Jn. 1: 18). The Son, whom John, Hebrews and the New Testament as a whole think of as taking flesh, is *the* Son of God.

(b) The passage in Hebrews in no way denies that God has spoken elsewhere than in Jesus. On the contrary, it affirms that he has. We shall see later that faith, at least, can rejoice with the Psalmist that 'The heavens tell out the glory of God, the vault of heaven reveals his handiwork' (Ps. 19: 1). But the specific point in Hebrews 1: 1,2 is that there had been a preparation for Christ in the history of God's ancient people, Israel. But 'when the fulness of time was come'—that means, 'at precisely the right moment from the point of view of God's eternal purpose'— 'God sent forth his Son' (Gal. 4: 4, A.V.) The prophets were by no means without effect. Their messages, though fragmentary, were given to them by God and owned by him. The psalmists and the best of the priests and kings had all been his faithful witnesses. But now he who was with the Father from eternity has come. The promise of the Old Testament is fulfilled in the New, and it is 'the measure of His greatness, and that which constitutes His glory, that He has been prepared to stoop so low and in fact has done so' (R. H. Lightfoot).

> 'And will this sovereign King
>   Of glory condescend?'

Isaac Watts never penned a question which expected a more emphatic answer 'Yes!' The Christian, then, can overlook neither the preparation for Christ, nor the finality of Christ; and by 'finality' I mean not that God has said and done nothing since the first century, but rather that God will never speak more clearly, or act more decisively, than he has in Christ: 'The finality of the Christian revelation is marked not by its temporal incidence alone, but by the transcendent character of the Person, the rank, the status, and the authority of Him through whom and in whom it comes. Here is not a prophet but a Son, who as the Messiah of God is the Lord of history, the divinely appointed Inheritor of the ages' (William Manson). Having seen him we have seen the Father (Jn. 14: 9). All the rest is commentary.

God makes himself known in Christ. But where do we find Christ? There are two answers to this question. First, we find Christ in the Bible; and the Bible will always be of crucial importance for Christians because it is, as Luther said, 'the cradle of Christ.' A distinguished Victorian scholar put it in this way: 'If I am asked why I receive Scripture as the Word of God, and as the only perfect rule of faith and life, I answer with all the fathers of the Protestant Church: Because the Bible is the only record of the redeeming love of God, because in the Bible alone I find God drawing near to man in Christ Jesus, and declaring to us in Him His will for our salvation. And this record I know to be true by the witness of His Spirit in my heart, whereby I am assured that none other than God himself is able to speak such words to my soul.' But these words of Dr Robertson Smith indicate also the second place where Christ is to be found. In the Bible, yes; but also *within*. By His Spirit God addresses us through the Bible in such a way that it is no antiquarian book to us; Christ is not locked between its covers. Far from it: a *living* Christ is presented to us and conveyed to us. By the Spirit he lives in our hearts (and not only, as Calvin comments, on our tongues or in our intellects) through faith (Eph. 3: 17). There is real point (even if, as we shall see, there is not the basis of a logical demonstration of God's existence) in A. H. Ackley's evangelical chorus:

> 'You ask me how I know He lives?
> He lives within my heart.'

After all, God's purpose in Christ is not simply to give us information about himself in response to which we might say, 'How interesting!' or 'Fancy that!' Christianity is no new philosophy; it is a new life which grows out of a new relationship with God which involves our whole being. It is a life of restored fellowship with God, of ever deepening commitment to our fellows in the Church, and of ever more zealous service to the world for God's sake. With sins forgiven and hope assured we march towards a wonderful goal. 'Now we see only puzzling reflections in a mirror'—but they *are* reflections of the truth; *then* we shall see face to face, and know as we are known (I Cor. 13: 12). Let me underline Paul's important point concerning our knowledge of God.

God has not left himself without a witness. We know him in Christ. But our knowledge, though true, is partial. It must be so, for we are mortals. God alone knows himself as he fully is; our minds just cannot contain him:

> 'Can you fathom the mystery of God,
> Can you fathom the perfection of the Almighty?'
>   (Job 11: 7)

But at first sight Zophar was wrong to continue, 'You can know nothing' (v. 8). We must take this as a dramatic way of saying, 'Compared with all that God is, what can *we* know?' For we can know enough. 'You may know God,' said Richard Baxter, 'but not comprehend him.' His older contemporary Richard Sibbes agreed: 'We shall apprehend Him, but not comprehend Him.' But a third Puritan, John Mason, put the point in as balanced and accurate a way as I have seen: 'We may truly conceive of God, though we cannot fully conceive of Him. We may have right apprehensions of Him, though not an exact

comprehension of Him.' Face-to-face communion with God is a
privilege reserved for believers in the world to come. Not for us
in this life that closeness of contact with God that Moses was
said to have had (Num. 12: 8). But Paul affirms that such
knowledge—knowledge which means union, fellowship, and not
simply intellectual grasp—will come. 'O glorious change!' cried
Matthew Henry, 'To pass from darkness to light, from clouds
to the clear sunshine of our Saviour's face, and in God's own
light to see light! It is at best but twilight while we are in this
world; there it will be perfect and eternal day.' Here lies the
Christian's hope; from here he draws daily his strength and
consolation.

I

I have begun resolutely with Christ. He is Christianity's
distinctive datum. How can a Christian think of God without
thinking of the Christ who makes God known? We must
recognise, however, that some Christians, including many of the
most able Christian minds, have sought to begin elsewhere.
True, they have generally done this for apologetic purposes;
that is, they have either been attempting to justify their beliefs,
or to help men reach God by the path of reason. I shall briefly
give my reasons for thinking that we cannot reach the Christian
God by the path of argumentation, and then I shall develop the
positive points I have already made.

I am by no means saying that Christianity has nothing to do
with reason; that it is irrational, or concerned only with
emotions, and so on. The Christian is challenged to give a
reason for his hope (I Pet. 3: 15); there is everything to be said
for the attempt to show that the Christian approach makes
better sense of facts and of life than any other world view. I am
making the much more limited, but none the less important,
claim that we cannot devise a conclusive, coercive, knock-down,
logical demonstration of God's existence such that only a fool
would dissent from it. This is by no means to suggest that all
those who have attempted 'proofs' have been wasting their time.
At the very least they have bequeathed to successive generations

of students excellent material on which to sharpen their philosophical teeth. But more than that: they have drawn attention to factors such as the widespread consciousness of God, the sense of order and purpose which many detect in the world, the claim of the moral, the fact of experience—and all of these items have to be duly accounted for in any satisfactory view of the world. The somewhat forbidding philosopher Kant, stern critic of the traditional 'proofs' that he was, nevertheless declared that 'the starry heavens above me, and the moral law in me are two things which fill the soul with ever new and increasing admiration and reverence'. I come, then, to three points about the arguments for the existence of God which together will reinforce my conviction that the Christian must begin with God-in-Christ.

(a) None of the arguments has the status of a valid demonstration of the existence of God. The intellectual wrestling of Socrates, Plato, Aristotle, Cicero and many others is clear evidence of the claim of the God-question on the minds of men who lived before Christ. This interest has continued unabated in the Christian era, and we find that many Christians have held that man, being a rational creature can, by exercising his reasoning powers, produce a demonstration of the existence of God. They have not claimed that by this means a full and rounded picture of God is reached. On the contrary, they have been content to arrive at a Being, a Creator, a Cause, and to call this kind of theology which utilises man's native and natural gifts, natural theology. For information about God apart from the bare news that he exists, we are dependent upon revelation. By revelation we learn that God is triune, that he loves us, that he is Father, and so on; and the theology which treats of these themes is called revealed theology. This distinction between natural and revealed theology is one which has appealed to Catholic and Protestant alike, and the most competent of those who have utilised it have never spoken as if truth is divisible. That is, they have not taught that something can be true in philosophy and false in theology, or *vice versa*. On the contrary, the greatest of the natural theologians, Thomas Aquinas, maintained that a truth acquired by reason could not conflict with one given in revelation; and he spoke for many when he said that 'the existence of God and other like truths about God which can be known by natural reason are not articles of faith, but are preambles to the articles'. The natural-revealed distinction has often come to the fore when Christians have been intent upon defending their position against attack, or upon persuading others of the validity of their claims. The 'natural' has been thought of as providing common ground as between believer and unbeliever, on the basis of which further enquiry could proceed.

Some, like Anselm, have begun from the idea of an infinitely perfect being which we have in our minds, and have argued that there must be an existing reality which corresponds with this idea. But it is a big 'must'; and the argument is circular: if we *begin* from the idea of a perfect being, it is hardly surprising if he is there in the conclusion to our argument! Others, like Aquinas, have argued from our experience of causation to a first cause, and from our experience of motion to a Prime Mover. But why a first cause? Why not an infinite regress? May not the universe just be a brute fact? As for Aquinas's suggestion that we may, from the evidence of design in the world, conclude to a Designer, why *one* Designer only? Why not a team of them? And what price a Designer who makes such a muddled world, in which, for example, so much apparently random and pointless suffering occurs?

More recently some have inferred God from our experience of being under moral obligation; but it is an inference only, not a strict, coercive proof. And most of us are sufficiently aware of our ability to 'tame' our conscience to be on our guard against the suggestion that the 'voice of conscience' is always and necessarily to be equated with the voice of God. Finally, some have argued from religious experience to God. The trouble here is that people experience all kinds of things, some of them very odd indeed. If, then, somebody says, 'I know there is a God because I have experienced him in my life,' he is testifying—a perfectly proper thing to do—but as a strict proof his claim fails. And as far as the sceptic is concerned, he is only telling us something about his psychological state. He is not demonstrating God's existence.

Some have sought to salvage what they can of the 'proofs'. Robert Flint, for example, said that whilst you can easily snap one rod, you cannot so easily snap a bundle of rods. In other words, the arguments for God's existence have a cumulative force even though each one on its own fails. Sadly, if we change the metaphor we can see that six broken signposts do not point the direction any more clearly than one! As for those who say that the proofs, though not conclusive, show that God's existence is probable—well, I do not think the Christian will be content with a situation in which the most he can say is that it is probable—or, at least, not altogether improbable, that God exists.

To repeat what I said earlier: the 'proofs' give us a forcible reminder that there are fundamental notions such as causation, purpose, the moral, experience and the like which clamour to be anchored within a coherent world view. Christians believe that the best home for these notions is within a theistic frame of reference, but they do not arrive at God by a process of discursive reasoning. God gives himself, and faith—also his gift—is a response to his gracious initiative; and it brings with it assurance.

(b) The 'proofs' do not yield the *Christian* God. They do not necessarily yield a worshipful, or even a pleasant, being. Professor H. D. Aiken put it pungently: 'Logically, there is no reason why an almighty and omniscient being might not be a perfect stinker.' There is something very impersonal about a First Cause or a Prime Mover; and it is not easy to see how the transition can be made from these to the kind of God in whom the Christian believes. As Harry Emerson Fosdick once wrote with the biologist Haeckel's suggestion in mind, it must be extremely difficult to *pray* to Mobile Cosmic Ether! The Puritan Stephen Charnock had much earlier put the general point in a nutshell: 'What comfort can be had in the being of God without thinking of him with reverence and delight!' It is not without significance that Professor Norman Malcolm, to whom more than to any other we owe the impetus to fresh thinking on the ontological argument, has recognised that the most impeccable argument would not lead anyone to belief in God in the Christian sense of the words. The question, 'Canst thou by searching find out God?' (Job 11: 7, A.V.) always receives a negative answer. As Pascal knew, the religious man does not worship *'le Dieu des savants et des philosophes*;' and, as a matter of fact, none of those who set forth 'proofs' found God for the first time at the end of their proofs. Most of them knew him already, and if they did not they were philosophers engaged in what was to them an hypothetical exercise. Of course, 'Seek and you shall find' is a command from Jesus himself (Matt. 7: 7). We must do it. But the strange thing is that having searched we do not find ourselves in the self-congratulatory mental state of those who at last have found Being; rather, we kneel humbly and gratefully as those who have *been found* by a Saviour:

> 'I sought the Lord and afterward I knew
>   He moved my soul to seek Him, seeking me;
> It was not I that found, O Saviour true;
>   No, I was found by Thee.'
>
> (*The Pilgrim Hymnal*, 1904)

(c) By concentrating on the 'proofs', and upon 'things cerebral' in general we can miss the point. It has often been pointed out that the Bible assumes God, it nowhere attempts to prove that he exists. It teaches us that all men are made in God's image; they bear his creative impress; they have his law written in their hearts. But these things they wilfully suppress, and they are therefore 'without excuse' (Rom. 1: 20). The Bible teaches too that God is to be seen in the things that he has made. The heavens *do* declare his glory. But the Psalmist does not think of the works as leading him by logical steps to the Creator-God. The works are God's to start with, so to speak. 'The Psalmist only saw repeated on the heavens what he already carried in his heart' (A. B. Davidson). But although God's handiwork is there for all to see, men will not see—the first book of Calvin's *Institutes* contains the classic statement along these lines. Now Vanity Fair comes in many different guises and it is a sobering,

if not altogether an awe-inspiring, thought that in certain
circumstances there may be little to choose between the cry of
'Q.E.D!' on completing one's 'proof', and the cry of 'Bingo!' on
completing one's card! Things intellectual can constitute a
splendid diversion. As the Victorian evangelist Brownlow North
said,

> 'I believe there are numbers of what are called learned and
> deep-thinking people, who profess to believe in God, and
> who would be troubled in their minds if they thought they
> were not honouring God, whose God in reality is no better
> than an idol of their own creation. They believe the
> revelations of their own intellect, rather than the re-
> velations of Scripture; and while they acknowledge a God
> of the universe, a God of nature, a God of creation, they
> know nothing of the only living and true God, the God of
> the Bible.'

If a man is truly (though not comprehensively) to know *that*
God he must first be known, found, by God (Gal. 4: 9). This
entails a transformation, a re-orientation of his self (Gal. 1: 16);
and the gospel, the good news, is that by grace through faith
such transformations can occur. The opening of the eyes is prior
to the assent of the mind; the former is God's work, the latter is
part of our grateful response.

So it transpires that of all creation's wonders we may say,
'These are but the outskirts of his ways; and how small a
whisper do we hear of him' (Job 26: 14); or with Watts we may
agree that whilst

> 'The heavens declare Thy glory, Lord,
>   In every star Thy wisdom shines,'

nevertheless,

> 'Thy noblest wonders here we view
>   In souls renewed, in sins forgiven.'

As for the manward side: it is ever the child-like, the pure in
heart, the humble, who see God (Lk. 18: 17; Matt. 5: 3,8; 11:
25; I Cor. 1: 19-31).

I am not at all surprised that John Henry Newman said of the
arguments for God's existence that 'they do not warm or
enlighten me; they do not take away the winter of my

desolation, or make my moral being rejoice'. How could they? And even if they were flawless as arguments there would still be man's rebellion between him and God, as the authors of the Westminster Confession realised:

> 'Although the light of nature, and the works of creation and providence, do so far manifest the goodness, wisdom, and power of God, as to leave men inexcusable; yet they are not sufficient to give that knowledge of God, and of his will, which is necessary unto salvation.'

God took further steps in Christ. So it comes about that

> 'Our proof of Him is little more than setting forth in an orderly or impressive way the situation or experiences in which He is borne home on us. It is not a case of syllogism but of observation and experience . . . Our certainty of God can only be based on the approach and action of the power which alone can set up the real relation between God and man. And that is God himself. God thought before we did, and He moved first'.
>
> (P. T. Forsyth)

Augustine puts the moral: 'Seek not to come to Him by any other way than Him. For if He had not willed to be the way, we should ever stray.' God save us from putting the intellectual cart before the gospel horse.

II

So I come full circle. I wish to underline two points made at the outset, and to conclude this chapter with one new, and very important point.

(a) God makes himself known, and if he did not we should not be able to know him. There *is* an objective revelation of himself in the things he has made; but that it *is* he who has made them—and us; and that he loves us: these things are disclosed to the eye of faith. And, paradoxical though it may seem, the very faith by which we apprehend is *also* a gift to us from him. 'It is God's gift, not a reward for work done' (Eph. 2: 9). All is of grace: 'Religion begins with a revelation that comes down, not a passion that goes up' (P. T. Forsyth). The wonder is that 'God, mighty and mysterious, gives himself to be our God' (*Declaration of Faith* of the Congregational Church in England and Wales, 1967). Grace—God's loving offering of himself in fellowship to man—was his free act from the moment of creation; in face of the ugliness of man's perversity and sin, grace is doubly gracious. Still he comes, his hand outstretched. Unlike Aristotle's aloof deity our God is intimately concerned with moral matters. Like the father of the prodigal he runs to meet the sinner (Lk. 15: 20) By his self-giving in Christ he bears our shame and vanquishes our sin; he restores the fellowship we have broken. When we are morally unable to grasp the things of the Spirit (I Cor. 2: 14) he takes the scales from our eyes, so that like the blind man whom Jesus cured, though with deeper meaning, we can testify, 'Once I was blind, now I can see' (Jn. 9: 25). We do not say that arrogantly, as if it were our triumph; we know that we can only say it at all because of his triumph. It is a joyful claim, but how humble it makes us feel! We are not here in the realm of argument, but of grace. It is not a question of intellect and logic, but of fellowship and will. The intellectual question pales into insignificance before the moral one. The worst that the intellectual question can do is to give us a headache, or to encourage us to fiddle while Rome burns. But our moral condition causes us to stifle the truth (Rom. 1: 18), and brings God a Cross. His coming to meet the lowest of his prodigals takes him *so* low; and having come, he acts in a way that the father in the parable never did: he not only forgives, he atones. There, supremely in the Cross-Resurrection event we see our God, and see him in action. But already we have come to our second point.

(b) God makes himself known in history, and supremely in Christ. To Christians history is not, as it is to Hindus, *maya*, illusion. It is the theatre of God's gracious activity. The Bible tells of his dealings first with his ancient people, Israel, and then with his New Israel, the Church. Whether old or new, his people were called by him to be the agents of his love and purpose in the world. The call is to service, not to favouritism—a distinction which God's people, whether ancient or modern, have not always been very good at making (hence e.g. Amos 3: 2; Jas. 1: 22).

God works in history, and within history he has made himself known in many ways: through prophet, priest, king, psalmist, apostle. All these have spoken at his behest. But God, being a God of action and not of words only, has done decisive deeds as well. The Bible records three paramount occasions of his saving activity. There is first the deliverance of Israel from bondage in Egypt (Exod. 20: 2; Deut. 11: 2-7; Amos 2: 10, etc.); next, there is the divine judgment upon God's wayward people which led to the Babylonian captivity, and to the eventual return of a remnant of the people (Ezra 1; Neh. 2); and finally there is God's coming in human form in the person of his Son (Gal. 4: 4, A.V.). In the first the reference of the saving event is relatively localised (e.g. Ps. 81: 10); in the second the restoration of the people is with a view to universal mission (Isaiah 60: 3); but in Christ we are confronted by God's revelation in its fully cosmic proportions: 'In him everything in heaven and on earth was created, not only things visible but also the invisible orders of thrones, sovereignties, authorities, and powers: the whole universe has been created through him and for him. And he exists before everything, and all things are held together in him' (Col. 1: 16,17). Then comes the really stupendous claim: 'in him the complete being of God, by God's own choice, came to dwell. Through him God chose to reconcile the whole universe to himself, making peace through the shedding of his blood upon the cross—to reconcile all things, whether on earth or in heaven, through him alone' (Col. 1: 19,20). Such is the testimony of Paul, the erstwhile enemy of the Cross, as he viewed with hindsight *the* saving event.

If all this is so, there are two main pitfalls to be avoided:

(i) We must never attempt to drive a wedge between the teaching of Christ and the Cross of Christ. His words and works belong together; his claims for himself are borne out by his actions. He is not just a teacher—even the best there ever was. He is not one who informs us about a revelation of God; he is not even one who brings us a revelation from God. He *is* God's revelation: 'In the Scriptures there is a draught of God, but in

Christ there is God Himself. A coin bears the image of Caesar, but Caesar's son is his own lively resemblance. Christ is the living Bible' (Thomas Manton). Or, more poetically:

'My dear Redeemer, and my Lord,
    I read my duty in Thy word;
But in Thy life the law appears
    Drawn out in living characters.'

(Isaac Watts)

(ii) We must not sever the Christian experience from its historic roots. Sadly, such theologians as Barth, Bultmann and Tillich, have been in danger of disengaging the gospel from history in all its ambiguity and messiness. We must maintain that the victory was wrought here below, once for all. Any sitting loose to that fact, whether in the interests of ideal history, existentialism, or theory of language, bids fair to undermine the gospel:

'Christian faith is an illusion unless the Lord Jesus Christ not only appeared in history, as the Gospels teach and as Christians have always believed, but was at the same time an actual self-manifestation of God, God Himself incarnate, and now and ever living as God and man, the one and only Mediator between God and man, the guarantee of God's will and power to save man. Upon this faith the Church of Christ was founded at the first, and in and by this faith it has always lived. In proportion as this faith has been weak and lacking, it has invariably languished and died.'

(John Dickie)

Doubtless God could have made the nations tremble (Isa. 64: 1,2); he could have saved by some other means—by deifying man, perhaps; he could have created creatures who were unable to doubt him and unable to disobey him; but he did not. He graciously made us; we grievously rebelled; he graciously saves. So it is that 'the Christian Gospel announces not an ascent of humanity to the heights of the divine in a transfiguration, an apotheosis, a deification of human nature, but a descent of the Godhead, of the divine Word, to the state of bondage of the purely human' (Karl Adam). With all due respect to the contemporary Catholic theologian, Paul said it much better and much earlier: 'Bearing the human likeness, revealed in human shape, he humbled himself, and in obedience accepted even death—death on a cross. Therefore God raised him to the heights and bestowed on him the name above all names, that at the name of Jesus every knee should bow...' (Phil. 2: 8-10).

In Christ we do *see* God, for he is

> 'God manifestly seen and heard,
>   And Heaven's beloved One.'
>
>   (Josiah Conder)

In Christ we do *hear* God, for

> 'God in the gospel of His Son,
>   Makes His eternal counsels known.'
>   (Benjamin Beddome and Thomas Cotterill)

But, above all, in Christ we have God *active* in his grandest work, the work of redemption:

> 'He bears our sins upon the tree,
>   He brings us mercy from above.'
>
>   (Thomas Kelly)

It is *God* in Christ who reconciled the world to himself (II Cor. 5: 19). Here as nowhere else we see God's active love:

> 'See where it shines in Jesu's face,
>   The brightest image of His grace;
> God, in the person of His Son,
>   Has all his mightiest works outdone.'
>
>   (Watts)

God's victory was not wrought in secret, or in the imagination, but for all to see. Small wonder, then, that in face of the powerful monotheistic tradition in which they had been reared, the early disciples called Jesus by the name hitherto reserved for God alone: Lord. No other title was big enough. 'Jesus is Lord' became their creed, their life, their battle-cry. So much for the reaffirmation of points with which I began. I come finally to my new, very important point:

(iii) To contemplate God's love; to know him by what he has done in Christ, is to be deeply moved. Emotion is not emotionalism, and there is no true Christianity without emotion. You cannot truly see what God has done—still less can you know it for yourself—and remain flint-like. Perhaps the greatest single peril confronting theologians, who so regularly handle sacred things, is that of not weeping enough. Even so,

> '... drops of grief can ne'er repay
>   The debt of love I owe:
> Here, Lord, I give myself away:
>   'Tis all that I can do.'

(Watts)

Yes indeed: to know God is to love him. 'Everyone who knows Him loves,' said Hugo of St Victor, 'and no one can love without knowledge.' To love God is to serve him, and to serve our fellows for his sake. It is to do his will. It is not just a matter of taking his name upon our lips—God's ancient people did that, and were trounced for it by Amos and Hosea; the rich man in Jesus's parable did that; he daily refused aid to the beggar at his gate—not that he did not see him (he called him by name from the place of torment). So he showed that although he was in Abraham's line, he was not a true son of Abraham (Lk. 16: 19-31). To love God is to do his will. As we do his will we learn more about him: 'Whoever has the will to do the will of God shall know whether my teaching comes from him or is merely my own,' said Jesus (Jn. 7: 17)—on which verse Matthew Henry commented, 'He that is inclined to submit to the rules of the divine law is disposed to admit the rays of divine light.' Christianity is a Way; and on the way we learn to know him who has first known us; to love him who has first loved us. As for our prospect, it is, by the grace of God, bright: 'his servants shall worship him; they shall see him face to face, and bear his name on their foreheads' (Rev. 22: 3-4).

* * * * *

A Hymn:

> O love of God! how strong and true,
>   Eternal and yet ever new;
> Uncomprehended and unbought,
>   Beyond all knowledge and all thought.
>
> O love of God, how deep and great!
>   Far deeper than man's deepest hate;

Self-fed, self-kindled, like the light,
  Changeless, eternal, infinite.

O wide-embracing, wondrous love,
  We read thee in the sky above;
We read thee in the earth below,
  In seas that swell and streams that flow.

We read thee best in Him who came
  To bear for us the cross of shame,
Sent by the Father from on high,
  Our life to live, our death to die.

We read thy power to bless and save
  E'en in the darkness of the grave;
Still more in resurrection light
  We read the fullness of thy might.

O love of God, our shield and stay
  Through all the perils of our way;
Eternal love, in thee we rest,
  For ever safe, for ever blest!

(Horatius Bonar)

A Prayer:

O Thou, Who art the Light of the minds that know Thee, the Life of the souls that love Thee, and the Strength of the thoughts that seek Thee; help us so to know Thee, that we may truly love Thee, so to love Thee that we may fully serve Thee, Whose service is perfect freedom; through Jesus Christ our Lord. Amen.

(*Gelasian Sacramentary,* source doubtful)

2
Abba, Father

Christ makes God known. But what kind of God does he make known? There are many possible answers to this question, for no single description of God tells all. The important point is that all our talk about God must be anchored in what we know of him in Christ; otherwise we shall arrive at an unworthy view of God. Why do we say of our God that he is love and not hate? Because of what we see in Christ. Why do we call him Saviour and not Destroyer? Because of what we see in Christ, and because of his redemptive activity in Christ. In this chapter, and in the rest of this book, we shall look at some of the ways of talking about God's nature and purpose. We may see only partially but, by grace, what we see is true.

I

One of the simplest words applied to God is 'Father'. We hear it so often; we take it for granted; but just reflect upon it! We are making the bold claim that he who framed the universe, who established the heavens, who set the rivers in their courses, he is our Father! The sublimest Person is given the most intimate and affectionate name, 'Abba', Daddy. It is not hard to understand why Celsus, whose god was far beyond everything conceivable, mocked Christians for their audacity. Undeterred, we call God Father because we have seen Jesus, and Jesus said, 'Anyone who has seen me has seen the Father' (Jn. 14: 9). There is something intimate about this seeing: it is not mere viewing. *Really* to see

Jesus is to know God. In the same way the words 'Our Father',
which Jesus taught his followers to use in prayer, are intimate
words. We are not onlookers; we are involved:

> 'I am His and He is mine
> For ever and for ever.'

(James G. Small)

In a communion sermon preached in 1861 Dr John 'Rabbi'
Duncan said, in words no less true for their now quaint ring,

> 'when thou comest to Christ, thou art come already to the
> Father; when thou seest Christ, thou hast already seen the
> Father. "I am feeble"—He is the Lord Almighty; "I am
> ignorant"—in Him are hid all the treasures of wisdom and
> knowledge; "I am in a low condition"—He is the Head of
> all principality and power; "Ah! but I am guilty"—Christ
> hath once suffered for sins, the just for the unjust. . . .
> Jesus is a suitable Saviour, a suitable Saviour to a lost
> sinner; for He is come to seek and to save that which was
> lost.'

Christians use the word 'Father' of God in a general way, and
in two very specific ways. God is Father in the general sense that
he is the creator of all. He is gracious to all besides. We must
never suppose that God, having created man, did not need to be
gracious until men sinned. His very act of creation was an act of
grace—of Fatherly, caring love. And even though his children
have rebelled against him he still graciously gives many gifts to
good and evil alike (Lk. 6: 35; *cf.* Matt. 5: 45). But when we use
the word 'Father' we do not primarily mean creator, begetter,
Father of the universe (true though those descriptions are). We
mean two particular things:

(a) God is 'the God and Father of Our Lord Jesus Christ'
(Eph. 1: 3 etc.). Jesus Christ is God's Son by right (Jn. 1: 1; 14:
11); he could by right call his Father by the affectionate name
'Abba' (Mk. 14: 36). It follows that he and no one else is
entitled to say that 'No one knows the Son, save the Father, and
no one knows the Father but the Son' (Matt. 11: 27; Lk. 10:
22). Nor is this knowing just 'knowing about'. It is mutual and
unbreakable union. He was with God from the first (Jn. 8: 58;
17: 5), and he it is of whom, at his baptism, God declares, 'Thou

art my Son, my Beloved' (Mk. 1: 11). With these words the Father owned and commissioned the Son (*cf.* Mk. 9: 7). It is interesting to note that the first and last recorded words of Jesus (prior to the Resurrection) have him referring to his Father (Lk. 2: 49; 23: 46)—we might say that he never thought of God in any other way; and this was certainly among the reasons why he so antagonised the Jewish leaders: 'by calling God his own Father, he claimed equality with God' (Jn. 5: 18).

The entire ministry of Jesus was performed in the knowledge that he was about his Father's business (Lk. 2: 49); that his deeds were pleasing to his Father (Jn. 8: 29); and that the Father was with him at all times (Jn. 14: 10). Even the cry of dereliction on the Cross (Matt. 27: 46; Mk. 15: 34) was as agonising as it was precisely because he was *the* Son. But God remained Father, and it was God in Christ reconciling the world to himself (II Cor. 5: 19). How natural then that having emerged triumphant from the valley of the shadow, Christ should commend his spirit into his *Father's* hands (Lk. 23: 46). 'The distinctive factor in Christianity,' wrote W. B. Selbie, 'is not that He thought God was the Father of men, but that God was *His* Father.'

(b) God is our Father, because by the Holy Spirit he has adopted a new family in Christ, so that we too are enabled to cry 'Abba! Father!' (Rom. 8: 15; *cf.* Gal. 4: 6). We know the Father through the Son, and all because of *saving* grace. Christ is Son by right; we are sons by adoption. All were born children; but not all are sons. Our ability to cry 'Abba' signifies our adoption by grace and our release from the power of sin so that we may now live new lives as the Father's sons (Gal. 4: 4,5; Jn. 1: 12):

> 'Thou art our Father now,
>   And we, Thy children dear,
> Adoring, in Thy presence bow,
>   With holy, filial fear:
> We love to own a Father's claim,
>   We glory in a Saviour's name.'

(George Grove)

Although we may on many occasions fall by the wayside, the Father calls us back; and so it is that our sonship continues into that Father's home of which Watts sang,

> 'There would I find a settled rest
>   While others go and come;
> No more a stranger or a guest
>   But like a child at home.'

Christ was never anything other than Son. God is never anything else but Father, and all worthy human fatherhood takes its cue from him (Eph. 3: 14,15). But men are not necessarily sons. For us sonship, a bare possibility, becomes actual through the Father's gracious redemptive work. In his only begotten Son he removes the barrier which prevents our sonship—that is the kind of Father he is. The prodigal's father forgives, and God's forgiveness is no less free; but the Father-God atones: 'God loved the world so much that he gave his only Son, that everyone who has faith in him may not die but have eternal life' (Jn. 3: 16). To be a son is to be *at-one* with the Father; it is a relationship into which we are adopted by grace. Outside his mercy once, we have now received his mercy (I Pet. 2: 10).

> 'Behold the amazing gift of love
>   The Father has bestowed
> On us, the sinful sons of men,
>   To call us sons of God.'

>   (The Psalter, 1781)

But if God's Fatherhood is universal, may we not catch glimpses of it apart from Christ, and especially before Christ? Certainly we may. It is quite wrong to suggest that before Christ nobody ever thought of God as Father. In Old Testament times God was understood to be the Father of his chosen people, Israel (Deut. 32: 6; Ps. 103: 13; Isa. 63: 16; 64: 8; Jer. 3: 4,19; 31: 19; Mal. 1: 6; 2: 10); and Israel was understood to be God's son (Exod. 4: 22; Deut. 14: 1; 32: 19; Isa. 1: 2; Jer. 31: 20; Hos. 1: 10). This fatherhood is a gracious fatherhood based upon a covenant relationship which God has initiated with his people. In a special, unmerited way they are his. But the prevailing emphasis upon God's sovereign holiness suffices to exclude, even from the Psalms, the intimacy of 'Abba'—'He is like a father more than He *is* a father' (P. T. Forsyth; *cf.* Ps. 103: 13). Jesus's prayer that his friends might be in him as he is in the Father (Jn. 17: 22,23) betokens a degree of warmth and union in the Father-Son-sons relationship which is found nowhere else. The wonder is that God is no less sovereign for being *our* Father! 'He is not only, as a Father, willing to help us, but as a heavenly Father, able to help us . . . He is a Father, and therefore we may come to him with boldness, but a Father in heaven, and therefore we must come with reverence.' (Matthew Henry)

II

The sad thing is that so many seem willing to settle for something less than sonship. I am not now thinking of honest atheists and agnostics, whose position deserves to be taken with the utmost seriousness, but of those who *do* believe in a certain rather unspecified 'something'. They do not believe that the universe is the product of blind chance. They think that there must have been a begetter of some sort. They rejoice in beauty and truth wherever they find them, and they think that these qualities are part of the *order* of things. They often have a highly developed moral sense which makes them so urgent in the pursuit of neighbourliness and the relief of suffering as to put some Christians to shame. They will even accept much of Christ's teaching (though the grounds on which they think he was correct in his moral principles and wrong in all his claims about himself are not usually made very explicit). But they will not, or at least they do not, see the Father through the Son. In the last resort their god is a force or a principle, not a person.

The consequence of this is that although they may value human love very highly, there is no place for love in their 'something'. Having no God to love, and having no consciousness of having been loved by God, their human love can all too easily be stretched to breaking point. The evidence for this is in any psychiatrist's consulting room, on any social worker's file;

and on the widest scale the evidence is war and man's inhumanity to man.

Christians believe that God as Father of all favours his children in countless ways. He gives our daily bread; he makes possible noble deeds; to him we owe the simple pleasures of the sunset and the song of the birds. We are glad that there is music and art—even if we cannot appreciate all of it. The talents, the ingenuity, the achievements, the endurance of men amaze and impress us. All of this, we believe, is the product of God's common grace: his favour shown indiscriminately to evil and good alike. All of these wonderful things go to make up what the Fourth Gospel calls our *bios* (life). This is our *mortal* life; all mankind shares it, and death ends it.

But what the God and Father of our Lord Jesus Christ desires is that as well as enjoying his temporal and human gifts, men should worship, serve and love him for ever. That is why he made them. He desires fellowship with us. He wants us to enjoy not only *bios*, but *zoë*, real life, new life. This new life is the Father's free gift to rebel children, and all who turn to the Father in humble trust and repentance may claim it. Apart from sin, common grace would have sufficed. It is a tribute to the blinding power of sin that so many who are quite happy to think in terms of a generating 'something' see no need of a Father-Saviour. God offers so much, and so often his best gift is spurned.

How would you feel if you continually tried to offer a promised gift to someone, only to have it thrown back in your face? Would you lose patience? Would you break your promise? Thank God that our heavenly Father is both patient and faithful. Let us think of each of these words in turn. We shall then see even more clearly the kind of Father Christ shows us.

III

Our Father God is patient. Israel had sinned. They had insulted God, broken the first commandment, and worshipped the golden calf. Moses interceded for the people, his words availed, and the covenant was renewed (Exod. 34). The terms in which God made himself known to Moses epitomise, among other things, God's patience: 'Jehovah, the Lord, a God compassionate and gracious, long-suffering, ever constant and true, maintaining constancy to thousands, forgiving iniquity, rebellion, and sin, and not sweeping the guilty clean away . . .' (Exod. 34: 6,7). God, said Matthew Henry, 'lengthens out the offers of his mercy;' or, as Tyndale rendered a parallel verse (Num. 14: 18), 'the Lorde is longe yer he be angrye.' The theme of the patience of God runs like a thread through all his dealings with his wayward people, and is well anchored in their hymns (Ps. 86: 15; 145: 8,9).

Incredible as it may seem, some have traded on the patience of God. They have understood it as giving them plenty of time to sin! Hence Paul's expostulation to the Romans: 'Do you think lightly of [God's] wealth of kindness, of tolerance, and of patience, without recognising that God's kindness is meant to lead you to a change of heart?' (Rom. 2: 4) Some have even suggested that God's failure to execute punishment is due to weakness. Stephen Charnock waxed vehement at the thought:

> 'Could he not make the motes in the air to choke us at every breath, rain thunderbolts instead of drops of water, fill the clouds with a consuming lightening, take off the reverence and fear of man, which he hath imprinted upon the creature, spirit our domestic beasts to be our executioners, unloose the tiles from the house-top to brain us, or make the fall of a house to crush us? It is but taking out the pins, and giving a blast, and the work is done. And doth he want power to do any of those things?'

It's all rather seventeenth-century! But we take the main point: 'It is not, then, a faint-hearted or feeble patience that he exerciseth towards man.' God delays neither in order to encourage sin, nor because he is powerless to act.

The patience of God is the grace of God allowing men time to repent and return to him. To presume upon his patience is both wrong and imprudent. Whilst 'he will not always chide, neither will he keep his anger for ever' (Ps. 103: 9), it is also true that 'though the patience of God be *lasting*, yet it is not *everlasting*' (William Secker). It cannot be otherwise, for God is a righteous,

moral God. But God voluntarily stays his hand. Nowhere does
this come out more poignantly than in the story of Hosea. The
prophet knew not only the agony of a broken marriage, but the
double agony of still loving the faithless Gomer who had
deserted him. How much more must God love his sinful people!
In chapter 11 of his book Hosea struggles to hold together the
idea that the righteous God must punish sin, and the idea that
the loving God agonises over his lost sons, Israel. The most
hopeful feature of the passage is the prophet's realisation that
God does *not* deal with us as we deserve; his grace and mercy
are far more than we could ever deserve. Whatever God may
have laid down in earlier times concerning strife between man
and man (Exod. 21: 24, etc.), he does not deal with us on the
basis of an eye for an eye and a tooth for a tooth. He comes, as
the Christian knows, to seek and to save the *lost*.

How patient God is! Before ever we think of turning to him,
and even when men never think of turning to him, he bestows
countless blessings upon us all. 'The worst of men partake of the
comforts of this life in common with others, which is an
amazing instance of God's bounty and patience.' (Matthew
Henry). And how graciously he treats those who do return.
There is no reproach; there is no 'Why did you do it?' There is
joy in heaven when a sinner returns (Lk. 15), and for us there is
full forgiveness:

> 'Far as east is from west,
>   so far has he put our offences away from us.'
>
> (Ps. 103: 12)

Forgiving is not only forgetting. Rather, it is the restoration by
God's grace of a relationship which we had broken. This is not
to say that we may not have to bear the consequences of former
sin. We have a new life, and with it comes the strength to
surmount any adverse legacy of the old life.

There are two things we can do. We can give thanks to God
for his patience which gives us so long a time for repentance (II
Pet. 3: 9). After all, 'We can never bless God enough for His
patience, that has kept us so long out of hell; nor for His mercy,
that so earnestly invites us to heaven' (John Mason). We can
join with F. W. Faber in singing,

'No earthly father loves like Thee,
    No mother, e'er so mild,
Bears and forbears as Thou hast done
    With me, Thy sinful child.'

Secondly, far from trading on the time his patience gives, we can use it aright:

'Come, let us to the Lord our God
    With contrite hearts return;
Our God is gracious, nor will leave
    The desolate to mourn.'
                    (Scottish Paraphrase of Hos. VI, 1781)

'Suck not poison out of the sweet flower of God's mercy. . . . To sin because mercy abounds is the devil's logic' (Thomas Watson).

IV

Our Father God is faithful. There are many ways of speaking of the faithfulness of God. I shall briefly mention four of them.

(a) God is faithful in keeping his promises:

'Faithful, O Lord, Thy mercies are,
    A rock that cannot move;
A thousand promises declare
    Thy constancy of love.'
                    (Charles Wesley)

God is utterly true to himself. 'If we are faithless he keeps faith, for he cannot deny himself' (II Tim. 2: 13; Heb. 10: 23; 11: 11). This God, who cannot lie (Num. 23: 19; I Sam. 15: 29) has promised eternal life long ages ago (Tit. 1: 2). Because *he* has promised it he will bring it to pass. God's promises, unlike those of the Evil One (Jn. 8: 44), are never broken. He is a rock (Deut. 32: 4 etc.), and his word 'endures for evermore' (Isa. 40: 8; I Pet. 1: 25). Christ is the Word made flesh; he shows us our faithful Father; he is and must be the truth (Jn. 14: 6). Hearing him we hear God; seeing him we see God; obeying him we obey God; loving him we love God. Because we are adopted as sons in him who is the truth, our sonship is assured and our hope is well founded; for Christ is the reliable witness (Rev. 1: 5; 3: 14;

19: 11) of the Father 'with whom is no shadow of turning' (Jas. 1: 17, A.V.). 'He is the Yes pronounced upon God's promises, every one of them' (II Cor. 1: 20). So it is that 'When other helpers fail, and comforts flee' (H. F. Lyte); when fears grip or sorrows descend, we may know with Watts that

> 'His very word of grace is strong
>   As that which built the skies;
> The voice that rolls the stars along
>   Speaks all the promises.'

(b) God is faithful in forgiving the sins of the penitent. This is his promise:

> 'Though your sins are scarlet,
>   they may become white as snow;
> though they are dyed like crimson,
>   they may yet be like wool.'

(Isa. 1: 18)

Or, in Matthew Henry's charming paraphrase, 'Though our sins have been as scarlet and crimson, a deep dye, though we have been often dipped, by our many backslidings, into sin, and though we have lain long soaking in it, as the cloth does in the scarlet dye, yet pardoning mercy will thoroughly discharge the stain.' Of the faithful Father it may truly be said that 'If we confess our sins, he is just, and may be trusted to forgive our sins and cleanse us from every kind of wrong' (I Jn. 1: 9).

Here we see that God's faithfulness is synonymous with his righteousness. God acts rightly; and he is consistent. If, then, we expect him to be faithful to his promise to forgive the penitent, we must not be surprised if he eventually punishes the impenitent (Zech. 1: 6). There is no opposition between God's justice and mercy, and we must never drive a wedge between them as if to say, 'God ought to be just, but fortunately he has decided to waive justice in favour of mercy.' In all things God acts rightly, in character. His mercy is his justice properly in action towards penitents. His punishment of the hardened impenitent is equally proper, and is light years away from revenge, spite, or petulance. Even so, the first word is love: 'Whom the Lord loveth he chasteneth' (Heb. 12: 6, A.V.; *cf.* Prov. 3: 11; Rev. 3: 19). A father who sat lightly to sin would not be *the* Father. It remains gloriously true, however, that God's greatest delight is to save, and that it is not his will that any be lost (II Pet. 3: 9).

(c) God faithfully keeps his people in this life: 'His truth for ever stands secure . . . And none shall find his promise vain' (Watts). It is not always easy to believe this. Life can be hard. But, as Paul reminded the Corinthians, 'so far you have faced no trial beyond what man can bear' (I Cor. 10: 13)—on which verse Matthew Henry commented, 'There is no valley so dark but he can find a way through it.' But it is *through* it, not around it. God takes us *through* the valley of the shadow (Ps. 23: 4), but he is there with us. The worthy Isaac Watts made no bones about it:

> 'True 'tis a straight and thorny road,
>   And mortal spirits tire and faint;
> But they forget the mighty God
>   That feeds the strength of every saint.'

We must never forget that our Saviour, *the* Son, was 'tested in every way' (Heb. 4: 15)—and how he was tested! He has a fellow-feeling with us. He is not unaware of our fears and anxieties; and we, by grace, are in him. We must not be surprised if we have to suffer—Paul did, and he counted it a privilege to suffer for Christ (II Cor. 11 *cf.* Phil. 1: 29); he knew too that 'I have strength for anything through him who gives me power' (Phil. 4: 13). Those who by nature are not the Father's sons cannot always be expected to look with favour upon those who, by grace, are. For all that, as the converted slave trader blurted out,

> 'His way was much rougher and darker than mine;
>   Did Jesus thus suffer, and shall I repine?'
>   (John Newton)

Above all, we must ever remember that the Son in whom we are sons is victorious! In him we are more than conquerers (Rom. 8: 37). This is what puts that defiant 'come what may' into the Christian faith. The outcome is assured, for the Lord, the victorious one, is to be trusted (II Thess. 3: 3). No wonder it is said of the true Christian pilgrim that:

'Hobgoblin nor foul fiend
    Can daunt his spirit;
He knows he at the end
    Shall life inherit.'

(John Bunyan)

This brings me to my final point.

(d) The faithful God may be trusted to bring all his sons to
their eternal home: 'He will keep you firm to the end, without
reproach on the Day of our Lord Jesus' (I Cor. 1: 8; *cf.* Rom.
8: 31f; Phil. 1: 6,10; Col. 1: 22). 'Mercy drew the covenant,' said
John Mason; 'faithfulness keeps it; mercy called us; faithfulness
will not cast us off.' Thus it may be said of God's true sons that
'on the Day of Christ you will be flawless and without blame,
reaping the full harvest of righteousness that comes through
Jesus Christ, to the glory and praise of God' (Phil. 1:10,11).

'O glorious expectation, when the faithfulness of God comes
in to support our hopes!' (M. Henry) What a great provider the
faithful Father is:

'Pardon for sin and a peace that endureth,
    Thy own dear presence to cheer and to guide;
Strength for today and bright hope for tomorrow:
    Blessings all mine, with ten thousand beside!

Great is Thy faithfulness!'

(Thomas O. Chisholm)

V

It almost seems as if the doctrine of the Fatherhood of God
was too much for some of the early Christian thinkers. The air
they breathed was not very congenial to the idea of an intimate
God. The Greek idea of a ruling, generating, universal, far-off
divine spirit was widely influential. Thus, long before Christ,
Plato could speak of God as the 'father and maker of the
universe,' and Epictetus referred to 'our good king and father.'
Language of this kind rolls easily off the tongue of the Christian
apologist Justin Martyr, to whom God is 'the Father of all and
the Ruler'; and Irenaeus characteristically thinks of Jesus as the
Logos—a word which to him suggests united wills rather than

warm fellowship. Again, Clement of Alexandria thinks of Christ mainly as a teacher, as when he declares, 'Illuminated we become sons; being made sons, we are made perfect; being made perfect, we are made immortal.' The suggestion is much more one of learning from a teacher, than of exulting in new life because of the grace and mercy of a Redeemer. Moreover, Clement thinks of God's love and sympathy as denoting a condescension on the part of one who in his inmost being is beyond the reach of such emotions.

Even so great a Christian thinker as Origen lost something of the personal intimacy of the Christian idea of the Father-God. For him the Son is the Father's Word (by which he means a rational principle), and his understanding of redemption is correspondingly intellectualist rather than moral and personal. True, he has much to say of God as the Father of the Second Person of the Trinity; but of God as Father of men we hear little. The Monarchians exalted the unity of God at the expense of his nearness, whilst the Arians thought of the Father almost exclusively as the begetter of the Second Person of the Trinity. Athanasius, who served the Church well in upholding the true relation of the properly divine Son to God the Father, did not go on to elaborate the sonship of men.

The influence of the Roman intellectual environment, and especially of Roman law, upon such men as Tertullian and Augustine made the concepts of law and sin loom larger in their minds than that of Fatherhood. So we proceed through the Middle Ages, with their disputes concerning nature and grace, freewill and predestination. But whatever positions men took up on these questions, the notion of Fatherhood was not formative. Increasingly God became sovereign will rather than Fatherly sovereign. Nor could the Reformers entirely redress the balance in their *theology* though, as is well known, in their religion their experience of the Father-God was of the deepest kind.

We may go so far as to say that it was not until the latter part of the nineteenth century that the twin ideas of 'the Fatherhood of God and the brotherhood of man' came to the fore—and then it was a mixed blessing. What was held to be theological clutter was, perhaps too quickly, swept aside by some; some had an unduly optimistic faith in man's ability to bring in God's kingdom (which, in fact, is always his gift); the distinction between men as children of God and men as sons of God was well-nigh obliterated; and the idea of the fatherly love of God was often sentimentalised and trivialised. His justice and righteousness were minimised and, as one writer put it, hell was frozen over or turned into innocuous ashes.

In face of all such tendencies we must remember that not all are sons, and that God is just. Sin is a reality, and some, sadly, are enemies of God. If that does not matter much to us, what kind of sons are we? It matters to God. It costs him the Cross. We must go on, therefore, to make plain the truth that the patient faithful Father whom the Son makes known to us is not the God of any-kind-of love. He is the Father-God of *holy* love. This must be our next theme.

* * * * *

A Hymn:

> 'Abba, Father!' we approach Thee
>   In our Saviour's precious name:
> We, Thy children, here assembling,
>   Now the promised blessing claim.
> From our sins His blood hath washed us;
>   'Tis through Him our souls draw nigh;
> And Thy Spirit, too, has taught us,
>   'Abba, Father,' thus to cry.
>
> Once as prodigals we wandered,
>   In our folly, far from Thee;
> But Thy grace o'er sin abounding,
>   Rescued us from misery.
> Thou Thy prodigals hast pardoned,
>   Loved us with a Father's love;
> Welcomed us with joy o'erflowing,
>   E'en to dwell with Thee above.
>
> Clothed in garments of salvation,
>   At Thy table is our place;
> We rejoice, and Thou rejoicest
>   In the riches of Thy grace.
> 'It is meet,' we hear Thee saying,
>   'We should merry be and glad,
> I have found my once lost children,
>   Now they live, who once were dead.'

'Abba, Father!' all adore Thee,
  All rejoice in heaven above;
While in us they learn the wonders
  Of Thy wisdom, grace, and love.
Soon before Thy throne assembled,
  All Thy children shall proclaim,
'Glory, everlasting glory,
  Be to God and to the Lamb!'

(James George Deck)

A Prayer:

O Lord, Father everlasting, in Whom is all we need or can desire; our hearts take comfort in the very thought of Thee; we have rest in the remembrance that we are Thine.

(S. T. Fraser, twentieth century)

3

Mercy Reigns, and Justice Too

'God is love' (I Jn. 4: 8,16). That is a mighty affirmation, and it is a true statement. But it is not an exhaustive definition of God. We have not said all there is to say about God when we have said that he is love. We have already seen that patience, truth and faithfulness are important qualities which he possesses in their perfection. 'God is love' means that whatever God does is expressive of love; he cannot act unlovingly; it is of his very nature to love. We might therefore be tempted to say that love is God's supreme quality. But what kind of love? 'Love' is a slippery, and sometimes a sadly devalued, word. It can be used sentimentally; it can mean almost the same as indulgence; it can stand for something spineless or it can stand for something strong. So I suggest that we need to think of God's love in relation to other qualities he possesses, and to understand them all in relation to Christ, the Son who shows us the Father.

When we contemplate God's love in Christ I think we see that it is, above all, holy love with which we have to do. God is the holy loving Father. This is another way of saying that 'Love can only be exercised by God when it is right love. Holiness is the track on which the engine of love must run' (A. H. Strong). The Christian gospel is that God the holy one acts towards the undeserving sinner in love. *That* is grace; *that* is good news.

If we do not think of God's love as holy love we shall be in danger of driving a wedge between God's justice and his mercy, his wrath and his grace. We shall conjure up inaccurate pictures of Christ the obedient Son pleading with God, the outraged

Father, to stay his justice, to sit light to sin, and to resort to benevolence; whereas in fact the Cross reveals a holy love which is satisfied, and which is victorious. It is not the Son *versus* the Father; it is God in Christ reconciling the world to himself (II Cor. 5: 19). But let us take one step at a time.

I

God's love is holy love. It is something quite other than upgraded human love. God's love has a depth and a quality which far surpasses all that we can conceive by the word 'love'. The Bible nowhere says that God loves like us. On the contrary, we are exhorted to love like him—to love as we have been loved (Jn. 15: 12,17). Jesus laid this obligation upon his disciples as he prepared to face the Cross. If we are to love like that we are under a new (*kainē*, 'fresh', not *nea*, 'novel') commandment indeed (Jn. 13: 34). It is by revelation alone, and not by the introspection of our own little love, that we begin to see how he has loved us. A man's love might prompt him to lay down his life for a friend, but 'Christ died for us while we were sinners, and that is God's own proof of his love towards us' (Rom. 5: 8).

Agapē is the special word the New Testament uses for this undeserved, overflowing love. It is to be distinguished from *eros*, which originally signified man's aspiration for the good and his union with the divine, but which by the first century had acquired sensual and degrading overtones; and it is much more than *philia,* brotherly love. It is love which is utterly self-giving even when—indeed, especially when—there is *no* worth in its objects. It is the love of which Paul speaks when he says, 'There is nothing love cannot face; there is no limit to its faith, its hope, its endurance' (I Cor. 13: 7). But more than that, it is a love which *does* something. There are only the makings of a gospel in 'God is love.' It is 'a precious truth, but affirming no divine act for our redemption. *God so loved that he gave . . . He gave*; it was an act, not only a continuing mood of generosity . . .' (W. Temple) The love of God is active holy love which purposefully goes to the Cross for the loved ones, and which there defeats all the forces hostile to it in a glorious, Christianity-making resurrection.

In my attempt to describe the love of God I have already made it clear that there are forces opposed to it which it must vanquish. Why can love not say 'anything goes'? Because God's love is not sentimental tolerance; it is holy. God is 'glorious in holiness' (Exod. 15: 11); he is in a class of one; and of that holiness Thomas Watson said that it is 'the most sparkling jewel in his crown.' It is what makes him *God.*

How can we probe such an area as this? P. T. Forsyth realised that

> 'When we are dealing with the holy . . . we are in a region which thought cannot handle nor even reach. We cannot go there, it must come here . . . The holy is both urgent and inaccessible. It is imperative, yet unapproachable. The situation is only soluble by a miracle. That is the miracle of Revelation, of Grace. The unapproachable approaches, enters, tarries, lives, dies, conquers among us and in us . . .'

A number of strands go into the Christian understanding of the holy. In the first place there is the idea of the holy as being that which is for ever apart from us, the 'wholly other'. This is what lies behind Reginald Heber's words,

> 'Only Thou are holy, there is none beside Thee,
>   Perfect in power, in love, and purity.'

God is unfathomable; he inspires awe—even dread. When Jacob awoke from his dream at Bethel he exclaimed, 'How fearsome is this place!' (Gen. 28: 17). He had been overcome by holy dread. When the sons of Jeconiah did not join in the rejoicing when the Philistines returned the Ark of the Covenant to Israel seventy of them were struck down. The response of those who witnessed this was, 'No one is safe in the presence of the Lord, this holy God' (I Sam. 6: 20). Again, the rash touching of the Ark, the holy thing, resulted in Uzzah's death (II Sam. 6: 6ff). It was this aspect of holiness, this 'tremendous and awe-inspiring mystery' which Rudolf Otto investigated in his classic work *The Idea of the Holy* (E. T. 1923). He found this sense of holy dread at the root of all religious experience, and he understood it as something non-rational, the 'numinous'. The numinous, said Otto, prompts in us a sense of 'creature-consciousness' and we feel utterly abased.

Otto's insistence upon the awe-inspiringness of God was a
timely rejoinder to the followers of Ritschl, who thought of the
holy in predominantly ethical terms. As Dr H. R. Mackintosh
said,

> 'If we reflect carefully upon what happens in our minds
> when we are in a specifically *reverent* mood, we can make
> out that reverence is not compounded merely of things like
> gratitude, trust, love, or confidence; for all these we might
> feel towards an exceptionally good man. There is
> something over and above; there is an awareness of the
> Holy One. To use a natural expression, we are
> "solemnized".'

But although Otto realised that we feel *unworthy* before this
mystery, his emphasis upon otherness and awesome dread does
not make it easy for him to accommodate the notion of the
moral holiness of a revealed God. Whereas sentimentalists feel
more at home with God's love than with his holiness, Otto
seems to exalt holiness at the expense of love. For my part I feel
more abased before holy, personal, near love, than before a
holiness which is remote and non-rational. So, I fancy, did
Isaiah when he 'saw the Lord' in the year that King Uzziah
died. The seraphim cried,

> 'Holy, holy, holy is the Lord of Hosts:
>   the whole earth is full of his glory;'

and Isaiah cried,

> 'Woe is me! I am lost,
>   for I am a man of unclean lips
> and I dwell among a people of unclean lips;
>   yet with these eyes I have seen the King, the Lord of
> Hosts.'

(Isa. 6)

There you have the almost painfully close holiness of God.

Far from being remote, God's holy love is outgoing. He
declares that he will make his holiness known to many nations:
'they shall know that I am the Lord' (Ezek. 38: 23; *cf.* 36:
22,23). The holy One comes increasingly close to the least and
the lowest, without in any way detracting from his transcendent
majesty:

> 'Thus speaks the high and exalted one,
>> whose name is holy, who lives for ever:
> I dwell in a high and holy place
>> with him who is broken and humble in spirit . . .'

Moreover, the holy One is *actively* present. He comes

> 'to revive the spirit of the humble,
>> to revive the courage of the broken.'
>> (Isa. 57: 15)

He will prove his holiness by gathering his scattered people (Ezek. 28: 25). Indeed, everything he does is for the sake of his holy name (Ezek. 36: 22). 'His love is not abated by His greatness, nor His greatness by His love. His holiness hinders Him not from dwelling with the poor in spirit' (John Mason).

The closer the holy God comes the more challenging are his words. God's holiness becomes shorthand for his purity, his righteousness, his moral demand. At first the challenge is to ceremonial purity: Israel must show that she belongs to the one true God by the faithful observance of *his* ceremonies, and by the avoidance of pagan worship in all its forms. The motive is to be gratitude. For God has brought his people out of Egypt (Num. 15: 41 etc.), and holy—that is, ceremonially pure— worship is to be the expression of their thanks and obedience (Deut. 7: 5,6).

The ethical demands of the holy God assume ever greater importance, as when Isaiah of Jerusalem names God 'the holy One of Israel,' and when Habakkuk speaks of him

> 'whose eyes are too pure to look on evil,
>> and who canst not countenance wrongdoing.'
>> (Hab. 1: 13)

When the supreme challenge, 'You shall be holy [not out of taboo fear]; for I am holy' (Lev. 11: 44) is taken into the New Testament context of God's holy love as revealed in Christ (I Pet. 1: 16; *cf.* Matt. 5: 48) we cannot but agree that 'we do not stand before God merely as the ethically imperfect before the ethically Perfect, but as the profane before the Holy' (Sydney Cave).

So crucial did Stephen Charnock believe the idea of the holy to be that he wrote of God that 'It is a less injury to him to deny his being, than to deny the purity of it; the one makes him no God, the other a deformed, unlovely, and a detestable God'.

II

Holy love is righteous love. John, exiled on the island of Patmos, had a vision of the victorious saints of God singing, 'Great and marvellous are thy deeds, O Lord God, sovereign over all; just and true are thy ways, thou king of the ages. Who shall not revere thee, Lord, and do homage to thy name? For thou alone art holy' (Rev. 15: 3-4). Again, Henry Downton, contemplating the theme of Psalm 101 from a Christian perspective, and echoing Revelation, writes,

> 'Of mercy and of judgment
>   To Thee, O Lord, we sing,
> O Father, Son and Spirit,
>   O great eternal King;
> For only Thou art holy,
>   For Thou art Lord alone,
> And mercy still and judgment
>   Are pillars of Thy throne.'

In Christian faith and experience these twin pillars stand together. Why? Because, as P. T. Forsyth said,

> '"God is love" is not the whole gospel. Love is not evangelical till it has dealt with holy law. In the midst of the rainbow is a throne. There is a kind of consecration which would live close to the Father, but it does not always take seriously enough the holiness which *makes* the fatherhood of the cross—awful, inexhaustible, and eternal, as full of judgment as of salvation.'

Yet many have tried to pull the twin pillars apart. Marcion, for example, opposed the righteous God to the good God, and for this he was roundly attacked by Irenaeus:

> 'Marcion therefore, himself, by dividing God into two, maintaining one to be good and the other judicial, does in fact, on both sides, put an end to Deity. For he that is the judicial one, if he be not good, is not God, because he from whom goodness is absent is no God at all; and again, he who is good, if he has no judicial power, suffers the

same as the former by being deprived of his character of Deity.'

In fact, the Father

'is good, and merciful, and patient, and saves whom He ought; nor does goodness desert Him in the exercise of justice, nor is His wisdom lessened; for He saves those whom He should save, and judges those worthy of judgment. Neither does he show Himself unmercifully just, for His goodness, no doubt, goes on before, and takes precedence.'

It is not, then, that God's holiness punished sin, and that afterwards his love, half apologetically, offers salvation. The holy love, in whose presence sin cannot stand, is the same holy love which saves. We are judged as well as saved by holy love. Holy love is righteous love, and to flout it is to suffer. 'Imagine a motor driven by a madman,' said Emil Brunner. 'He will not permit a wall to stand in his way. "I won't stand for that," he says, and opens the throttle wide and rushes against the wall. This is a simile for the man who is disobedient to God. He must simply dash himself to pieces against God's holiness.'

'Far be it from God to do evil
    or the Almighty to play false!
For he pays a man according to his work,
    and sees that he gets what his conduct deserves.'
                                    (Job 34: 10,11)

The holy God can no more sit lightly to sin than the faithful and true God can tell lies. Is not this the kind of God we really, in our heart of hearts, desire? Quite apart from the affront to God's holiness, would it not deny our manhood, our responsibility, if God were for ever to say to sinners, 'There, there: you didn't mean it; let's pretend it did not happen; let's put it down to the unfortunate environment in which you were raised...'. As Professor H. R. Mackintosh said, 'By being less stringent God would become not more loving but less divine.' If the gospel of God's grace is what it is, sin needs to be sinful, and my sins need to be mine. To continue to sin because God is love is practical atheism; it is saying that love is divorced from holiness and righteousness, and that means that *God* is no more.

The truth is that God is not Saviour despite the fact that he is

just. He is a just God and a Saviour (Isa. 45: 21; *cf.* Rom. 3: 26;
Hos. 2: 19f). 'Righteousness, transferred into a word of the
affections, is love; and love, translated back into a word of the
conscience, is righteousness; the eternal law of right is only
another conception of the law of love; the two principles, right
and love, appear exactly to measure each other' (Horace
Bushnell).

God's holy love is revealed by his law, enshrined in the Ten
Commandments, written in the hearts of men, and supremely
active at the Cross. God's love never fails, but his love is
righteous love; consequently,

> 'For ever firm Thy justice stands
>   As mountains their foundations keep.'
>
>   (Isaac Watts)

The law of God reflects the character of God. Like him it is
'holy and just and good' (Rom. 7: 12). God, having graciously
made a covenant with his people, *equally graciously* provides the
framework within which they are to live the covenant life. But
disobedient man sins, and then the law stands over against him
as a threat. Alienated from the Father, he cannot keep the law,
and—at least in his quieter moments—the law's penalties alarm
him. But there is not only the penalty of the law; there is the
grace of law. The law is a custodian to lead the sinner to Christ
(Gal. 3: 24). In other words, the sinner's inability to obey, to
walk in the way of holiness; his longing to be free from a
guardian become oppressive, drive him to the Helper and
Emancipator. 'The law was therefore given that grace might be
sought; grace was given that the law might be fulfilled'
(Augustine). Or, in John Mason's words, 'God hath written a
law and a gospel; the law to humble us, and the gospel to
comfort us; the law to cast us down, and the gospel to raise us
up; the law to convince us of our misery, and the gospel to
convince us of His mercy; the law to discover sin, and the gospel
to discover grace and Christ.'

So it is that the sinner finds that the same holy love which
established the law saves him into a new relationship with God
through Christ, the fulfiller of the law. Christ alone has satisfied

the legitimate demands of the law. He, once for all, freely offered the full, perfect and sufficient act of obedience to his holy Father, with the result that for the believer the penalty is annulled. This is not to say that the law is now redundant. It has not been cast aside. But it is no longer a threat. It is now a challenge to the new man; it is a guide for his new life; and to obey it is part of the believer's grateful response to the God who has so loved him. He can now, with the Psalmist's godly man, delight in the law of the Lord (Ps. 1: 2): he can join the Psalmist in singing,

'O how I love thy law!'

For to love the law is to love him whose it is.

When the law of God is flouted, holy love is revealed as wrath. Ritschl, who did so much to place love at the centre of theology could, sadly, find little place for the idea of the wrath of God. Yet we cannot expunge the concept without verging upon that unwholesome sentimentality which demeans God. Certainly God is not petulant or vindictive (and that is why I shall omit a verse which speaks of God's 'vindictive wrath' when I quote a hymn by Tucker shortly). We might properly say that God's holy love is *vindicative*: it vindicates itself; and we may say that God's wrath is holy love expressed against sin. Sinners God pursues with Fatherly love, but sin he will not and cannot tolerate. Sin is wilful rebellion against his holy love, and his wrath kindles against it, for 'God's love is the radiance of his righteousness; God's justice is the sternness of His love' (Robert Mackintosh). God's wrath is his holy love repudiating and condemning sin (Ezek. 18: 20; Ps. 1: 6, etc.). 'It is a fearful thing to fall into the hands of the living God' (Heb. 10: 31), for he is a 'consuming fire' (Heb. 12: 29). We see this side of God's love in Christ's holy indignation against the sin of those who profaned the temple; those who neglected the needy; and those who were religious hypocrites. But we see the same holy love loving *sinners* with an everlasting love (e.g. Matt. 21: 12; Mk. 11: 15; Lk. 19: 45; Jn. 2: 14; Matt. 25: 31-46; 6: 2; 7: 5). We see holy righteous love at work throughout.

A weather vane on a barn was inscribed with the words 'God is love.' A parson asked the farmer, 'Does that mean that God's love is as variable as the wind?' 'No,' replied the farmer. 'It means that whatever way the wind blows, God is love.' In all things, in all circumstances, holy love acts aright; it can do no other. God cannot be untrue to his nature, and whether in remuneration or retribution, the judge of all the earth does right (Gen. 18: 25; *cf.* Rom. 2: 6-8; 11: 22; II Cor. 5: 10). Leaving on one side the verse about vindictive wrath, we find that William Tucker, the cutler and ironmonger of Chard who exclaimed on hearing George Whitefield's declaration of the gospel, 'I heard and felt it too,' got most of it into these verses:

> 'Infinite grace! and can it be
>   That heaven's Supreme should stoop so low?
> To visit one so vile as me—
>   One who has been his bitt'rest foe?
>
> Can holiness and wisdom join
>   With truth, with justice, and with grace,
> To make eternal blessings mine,
>   And sin with all its guilt erase?
>
> O love! beyond conception great,
>   That formed the vast stupendous plan!
> Where all Divine perfections meet
>   To reconcile rebellious man!
>
> There wisdom shines in fullest blaze,
>   And justice all her rights maintains,
> Astonished angels stoop to gaze,
>   While mercy o'er the guilty reigns.
>
> Yes, mercy reigns, and justice too,
>   In Christ they both harmonious meet;
> He paid to justice all her due,
>   And now he fills the mercy-seat.'

The Dutch theologian Herman Bavinck may take us forward to our next point. He wrote, 'The motto, "Let justice be done though the world perish," contains an element of truth. Nevertheless, Scripture emphasises this much more beautiful thought: justice must be done that the world may be *saved*.'

III

Holy love is victoriously atoning love. There are so many ways of talking about the inexhaustible love of God. We have already seen that God's love is patient, faithful and holy. We might also say that it is merciful. The Hebrew words translated 'merciful' mean that God forbears and keeps covenant (*chesed*); that he has compassion for man (*racham*), and that he is kindly disposed towards man (*chanan*). This mercy is shown to all men, whoever they are, and whatever they have done or failed to do. It is God's loving kindness shown to all. This mercy never fails (Ps. 136 etc.); it is shown to those who reverence God (Exod. 20), but also to those who do not (Ezek. 16; 18: 32; 33: 11). The Psalmist sums it up when he says of God that 'His tender mercies are over all his works' (Ps. 145: 9, A.V.).

But Christian experience has not been able to rest content with 'mercy' understood as 'general favour'. It has gone on to think of mercy as forgiving love. The Father God goes out in search of his prodigal sons, and his forgiving love anticipates their repentance. This mercy, this favour shown to the sinfully undeserving, this overflowing love of God, is grace. It is free, voluntary, and quite unmerited: 'There is no reason to be given for grace but grace' (Ralph Venning). It is always surprising. The recipient of grace had no right to expect it. 'This is one of the greatest mysteries in the world,' said John Bunyan, 'namely, that a righteousness that resides with a person in heaven should justify me, a sinner on earth.'

> 'The wondrous mercy of a God
>   Saves an apostate race;
> Applies the balm of Jesu's blood,
>   And yields a sacred peace.'
>
> (Richard Burnham)

Who could have deserved, or earned such a thing? Richard Burnham himself could scarcely believe it. In the preface to the collection of hymns he prepared for his congregation he writes, 'Your pastor is the unworthiest of the unworthy; yet unworthy as he is, he humbly trusts, through rich grace, he has in some measure found that the dear bosom of the atoning Lamb is the abiding home of his immortal soul.' It is all of grace—as Toplady knew:

> 'Nothing in my hand I bring,
>   Simply to Thy Cross I cling...'

But why the Cross? Why the blood of Jesus? Because holy love is not only patient, faithful, merciful love; it is atoning love, and as atoning love it is victorious. It is not enough, either for God or for us, that sinners should be forgiven. It is not enough for God because his holiness must be satisfied; it is not enough for us because, as Forsyth insisted, mere remission would leave us with a mistrusting conscience—it would be too good to be true. The penalty must be cancelled; a new relationship must be made. The Son makes the offering we could never make; the Father, who made it all possible, receives it, vindicates his Son, and calls out new sons in him. Such is holy, atoning, victorious love.

Gone is any suggestion that God is a remote deity, beyond suffering. Holy love agonises over those who are estranged from it. A Central American translation of the Bible renders John 3: 16 thus: 'God so hurt in his heart that he gave his only Son...' That is grace; and that grace, as Easter assures us, is victorious. Nothing can keep from the Father those who are his sons through *the* Son:

> 'What can separate us from the love of Christ? Can affliction or hardship? Can persecution, hunger, naked-ness, peril, or the sword?... I am convinced that there is nothing in death or life, in the realm of spirits or superhuman powers, in the world as it is or the world as it shall be, in the forces of the universe, in heights or depths—nothing in all creation that can separate us from the love of God in Christ Jesus our Lord.'
>
>   (Rom. 8: 35,38,39)

The sixteenth-century English spiritual writer John Fisher piled image upon image in an attempt to grasp the glorious truth:

> 'Truly the mercy of our most mighty and best Lord God is great, and so great that it hath all measures of greatness. Sometimes trees are called great for their goodly and great

height. Pits be called great for their deepness. Far journeys
be called great because they are long. Streets and highways
be called great for their breadth and wideness. But the
mercy of God containeth and is measured by all these
measures of greatness, and not only by one of them.'
As Paul said, the love of God is broad, long, high and deep
(Eph. 3: 18); and as Matthew Henry commented, 'The
dimensions of redeeming love are admirable.' Let us reflect upon
each of these spatial adjectives in turn.

(a) The love of God is broad. It reaches to all sorts and
conditions of men. It loves them before they turn, and it asks
nothing but that they turn and come. It is not only—and not
always—for the 'religious'; it is especially for outcasts. Some of
the most searching of Jesus's teaching occurs in what T. W.
Manson used to call Luke's 'Gospel of the outcast' (Lk. 15-19:
the lost son, the poor beggar, the widow—they are all there).
And how, during his ministry, Jesus mixed and mingled with the
least and the lowest—and how some of the 'religious' muttered
about it (Matt. 11: 19; Lk. 7: 34)! When the religious apply
their measuring rods to their fellow men they can show how far
from the Kingdom they are. The prodigal's elder brother, who
had hardly been out of his father's sight, was miles away from
his heart. The grace of God really is free and unmerited, and it
goes out to all,

'For the love of God is broader
    Than the measures of man's mind;
And the heart of the eternal
    Is most wonderfully kind.'

(F. W. Faber)

The protestations of a Jonah will not avail. If God desires to
save heathen Nineveh, he will save it—with or without the aid
of his chosen people. God's people are to testify to God's grace;
they cannot apportion it. And when holy love smashes the
barriers which separate man from God, and man from man, it
ill behoves the people of God to rebuild those barriers.

(b) The love of God is long. It never fails. He has loved us
with an everlasting love (Jer. 31: 3). Human love can fade and
wither, but the love of God in Christ never fails. It is not a love

which depends upon fortunes, which may change, or which
expects perfect obedience if it is to continue. Love is eternal
because God is God. He never lets his people go. Since God's
love is

> '   strong and true,
>   Eternal, and yet ever new,'

Bonar could sing,

> 'Eternal love, in Thee we rest,
>   For ever safe, for ever blest.'

(c) The love of God is high. This brings to mind once again
the holiness of God's love. Burnham captures it so well:

> 'The Father is a holy God;
>   His holy Son he gave;
> Who freely shed atoning blood,
>   A guilty world to save.
>
> The Spirit brings the chosen race
>   A holy Christ to view;
> And while by faith they see his face,
>   Their souls grow holy too.
>
> In holiness the saints delight,
>   While here on earth they dwell;
> By faith they wrestle day and night,
>   More holiness to feel.
>
> The Holy Spirit leads them on,
>   His holy truth to know;
> Inscribes his laws in every son,
>   And works obedience too.
>
> He makes them feel the cleansing grace,
>   That flows through Jesu's blood;
> Unites in love the holy race—
>   The new-born sons of God.'

But as well as dwelling upon God's holy love, Burnham
rightly suggests that those who live by this high love are
themselves raised. It happened to Saul of Tarsus when he was
apprehended by the risen Christ on the Damascus road. Though
proud to be an apostle of Christ, he never felt worthy to be one
(I Cor. 15: 9-10). He had been a zealous persecutor of

Christians; he had hounded them to prison. So amazing was the change in him when he was raised by holy love that the Christians could hardly believe it (Acts 9: 20,21). A similar thing happened in the case of John Gifford. He was a Royalist major, and a dissolute. When he was converted his neighbours in Bedford were surprised, and more than a little suspicious. Yet this was the man who became a pastor—the very pastor who helped the questing John Bunyan to find his Christian feet. The raising is not, of course, always so dramatic; but it happens. To know that one is loved by the high and holy love of the Father God is to rise.

In a third sense, God's love is high in that it is for ever beyond our power to express. William Gadsby, one of the Lord's rough diamonds, whose dying words were 'Free grace, free grace, free grace!' knew this well:

> 'High beyond imagination
>   Is the love of God to man;
> Far too deep for human reason,
>   Fathom it it never can;
> Love eternal
>   Richly dwells in Christ the Lamb.'

(d) The love of God is deep. It is a resource which knows no limit; it is a bottomless well. There is enough grace and mercy for all. The love of God in Christ is inexhaustible:

> 'O the deep, deep love of Jesus!
>   Vast, unmeasured, boundless, free;
> Rolling as a mighty ocean
>   In its fulness over me.
> Underneath me, all around me,
>   Is the current of Thy love;
> Leading onward, leading homeward,
>   To my glorious rest above.'
>
>   (S. Trevor Francis)

Confronted by such love we are not surprised that Thomas à Kempis sang,

> 'O love, how deep, how broad, how high!
>   It fills the heart with ecstacy,'

or that Mary Shekleton prayed,

'It passes knowledge that dear love of Thine,
    My Jesus, Saviour; yet this soul of mine
Would of Thy love, in all its breadth and length,
    Its height and depth, its everlasting strength,
Know more and more.'

IV

Holy love is challenging love. It is so in at least three ways:

(a) Holy love challenges our commitment, our feeble love.
'What reward,' asked Bernard of Clairvaux, 'shall I give the
Lord for all the benefits that He has done to me? By his first
work He gave me to myself; and by the next He gave Himself to
me. And when he gave Himself, He gave me back *my*self that I
had lost. Myself for myself, given and restored, I doubly owe to
Him. What, though, shall I return Him for *Him*self? A thousand
of myself would be as nothing in respect of Him.' In more
familiar words,

'Love so amazing, so divine,
    Demands my soul, my life, my all!'

(Isaac Watts)

That is the challenge; and the deeper our consecration grows the
more we realise that it was holy love itself that prompted our
faltering response, 'For it is by his grace you are saved, through
trusting him; it is not your own doing. It is God's gift, not a
reward for work done' (Eph. 2: 8,9).

(b) Holy love challenges our way of life, and reorientates it.
We know that we are no longer our own; we are his—bought
with a price (I Cor. 6: 20; 7: 23). The Christian life is a grateful
response to that fact: 'Let Thankfulness to God thy Creator,
Redeemer and Regenerator, be the very temperament of thy
soul, and faithfully expressed by thy tongue and life' (Richard
Baxter). Our gratitude puts our obedience in perspective. We are
no longer slaves; we are free. The law is not a threat, we delight
to obey it. Not indeed that we are legalists. Far from it; we
know that we are not saved by rule keeping, or, indeed, by
anything that *we* do. On the other hand, we are not

antinomians: we do not discard the law of God on the shaky ground that we are no longer under law but are now under grace (Rom. 6: 15). That way lies licence, not Christian freedom, as is exemplified in the careers of such as 'Mousetrap' Ward of Birmingham who, in the eighteenth century declared that because he was under grace, not law, he need not pay for goods taken from shops; and that he had a right 'to all the women in the world if they gave their consent.' The antinomian thus divorces God's love from his righteousness. The Father's love is no longer *holy* love. The truth is that 'Thou hast an art above God Himself, if thou canst fetch any true pleasure out of unholiness' (William Gurnall). When Augustine wrote 'Love, and do what thou wilt,' he did not mean that all the brakes are off, but rather that we should do what is prompted by a love in harmony with the Father's holy love.

We are to love as we have been loved (Jn. 15: 12, 17; *cf.* I Jn. 4: 19). And we have been loved to the uttermost by holy love. A 'godly walk', as our fathers used to call it, will be part of our grateful response to holy love—a response itself made possible by grace. As we set out on our walk we shall remember that it is still the pure in heart who see God (Matt. 5: 8); and we shall remember too that such a 'walk' requires us to love the brethren. As to that, William Temple wryly commented, 'When the Church keeps the New Commandment, the world may keep the Old.'

(c) Holy love challenges us to testify. 'If every bird of its kind, as Ambrose says, chirps forth thankfulness to its Maker, much more will an ingenuous Christian, whose life is enriched and perfumed with mercy' (Thomas Watson). We must tell the tidings, not simply live them. I fear we sometimes take false comfort from the fact that actions are supposed to speak louder than words. They may; and our actions should always be consistent with our words, otherwise we are hypocrites. But speak we must! 'You that have been monuments of God's mercy,' said Watson, 'should be trumpets of praise.' God will show us how to do this work lovingly, humbly and uncensoriously. And if 'success' seems to elude us let us remember that we are called to be obedient, not 'successful', and that God alone can take the scales from men's eyes.

So ends my very inadequate account of the holy love of God which judges, atones and challenges. There is much more which might be said, but I will end with a further reference to Thomas Watson, one of my favourite Puritans. In the preface to one of his books he writes, 'There are two things which I have always looked upon as difficult. The one is, to make the wicked sad; the other is, to make the godly joyful.' The sincere contemplation of the holy love of the Father God should serve both purposes.

* * * * *

A Hymn:

'O what matchless condescension
    The eternal God displays;
Claiming our supreme attention,
    To His boundless works and ways.
His own glory
    He reveals in gospel days.

Would we view His brightest glory,
    Here it shines in Jesu's face;
Sing and tell the pleasing story,
    O ye sinners saved by grace;
And with pleasure,
    Bid the guilty Him embrace.

In His highest work, redemption,
    See His glory in a blaze;
Nor can angels ever mention
    Aught that more of God displays;
Grace and justice
    Here unite to endless days.

True, 'tis sweet and solemn pleasure,
    God to view in Christ the Lord;
Here He smiles and smiles for ever;
    May my soul His name record;
Praise and bless Him,
    And His wonders spread abroad.'

(William Gadsby)

A Prayer:

Give us to know, O God, that you have all power to defend us, all wisdom to direct us, all mercy to pardon us, all grace to enrich us, all righteousness to clothe us, all goodness to supply us, and all happiness to crown us; through Jesus Christ, our Lord. Amen.

(Based on words of Thomas Brooks)

4

Greatness Unspeakable Is Thine

A teacher whose ears had long been attuned to such words as 'omnipresence', 'omniscience' and 'omnipotence' asked his class to name three attributes of God beginning with 'o'. Quick as a flash a Cockney youth replied, ''oly, 'oly, 'oly!' If we may understand the lad to have meant 'holy love', then his reply was wiser than he knew. The very plan of this book assumes that if we do not begin from the holy love of God made known to us in Christ, we shall find ourselves in difficulties when we come to fill out our understanding of God. We should have no reason to suppose that an omnipresent God who was *not* holy love had our best interests at heart; omniscience divorced from holy love could be threatening in the extreme; and apart from holy love omnipotence could be sheer, and even hostile, power.

You may feel that what I have just said is so obvious that it is tedious to spell it out. The fact is, however, that at various points in the history of Christian thought attempts have been made to determine and to classify the attributes of God which have led to the isolation of those attributes from God's revelation in Christ. The Pseudo-Dionysius, for example, had a most lofty appreciation of the mystery of God. What could *we* say of *God*? Our words cannot begin to describe him. God is absolutely incomprehensible; he is 'pure nothing'; any attempt to name him demeans him. So it was that, despite God's revelation in Christ, the Pseudo-Dionysius ended up with a mysterious, undifferentiated deity, of whom nothing could be said. It is easy to see why those who have followed this particular mystic path have been charged with pantheism.

Of course our ideas can never circumscribe God; but this does not mean that we are in the position of the Greek philosopher Simonides. He was asked by Hieron of Syracuse 'What is God?' He asked for a day to reflect upon the question. At the end of the first day he asked for two further days; at the end of those he asked for four further days—and so on. The longer he thought about God the more incomprehensible God became. But part of what it means to say that man is created in God's image is that man *is* able to know and respond to God. Were it not so there could be no revelation, for no matter what God did there would be no one able to receive the revelation. Man can receive the revelation; there is nothing wrong with his intellect. If he does not receive the revelation it is not because he is incapable, but because he *wills* not to hear God's voice.

What then have Christians said about God when they have been open to him? Let us take a few soundings. The medieval Schoolmen reflected much upon God. They said that by the way of negation (*via negationis*) we may say what God is *not*. We can deny that he is limited and imperfect. Then by the way of eminence or climax (*via eminentiae*) we can say that God possesses all the perfections of his creatures, but to an infinite degree. Finally, by the way of causality (*via causalitatis*) we can attribute to God all the qualities needed to explain the existence of created matter and mind. The Schoolmen held that all these operations could be conducted by man as man; that is, they belonged to the realm of natural as distinct from revealed theology. Quite apart from revelation all these things could be said concerning God. There was no necessity, then, of beginning from God's revelation in Christ.

Martin Luther, famed for his *religious* insight into the ways of God with man, also encouraged theology along a new line when he protested that 'there is nothing more dangerous than to wander with curious speculations in heaven, and there to search out God in his incomprehensible power, wisdom and majesty, how he created the world, and how he governeth it. If thou seek thus to comprehend God, and wouldst pacify him without

Christ the mediator, making thy works a means between him and thyself, it cannot but be that thou must fall as Lucifer did, and in horrible despair lose God and all together.' His advice, therefore, was, that we should go straight to Christ: 'Embrace him, and cleave to him with thy whole heart, setting aside all curious speculations of the divine majesty, for he that is a searcher of God's majesty shall be overwhelmed of his glory. I know by experience what I say.'

It cannot be said that this lesson was well learned by every post-Reformation theologian. For example, although Calvin himself preferred 'a vivid actual impression' of God to 'empty visionary speculation', it was not long before some highly orthodox theologies were being penned in which the writers set out not from God's revelation in Christ, but from a rather abstract consideration of the divinely perfect Being and the attributes he must possess. They came to speak of attributes which belong to God's being alone (metaphysical or incommunicable attributes), and attributes of which there are analogies in human experience (religious or communicable attributes). The lists of attributes, and the names of the classifications, vary from author to author, but we generally find that independence, infinity, immutability, and unity are among the incommunicable attributes; and that omnipotence, omniscience, freedom, holiness and love are among the communicable attributes. In working out their accounts of God's attributes the older scholars generally piled up scriptural 'proofs' for their statements, and sometimes referred to the arguments for God's existence as being illustrative of the attributes.

The best of these scholars never lacked self-criticism. They sought to guard against the appearance of dividing God into two with their twin lists of attributes. They realised that the so-called incommunicable attributes must inform their understanding of the so-called communicable ones—God is *infinite* in *love*, for example; and they saw that the so-called communicable attributes were never in man in exactly the same way that they were in God. The Westminster divines of the seventeenth century said it all in one breath in their Shorter Catechism. In answer to the question, 'What is God?' (and I always think that the first word there encourages a degree of abstraction that 'Who' would not) they replied 'God is a Spirit, infinite, eternal, and unchangeable, in his being, wisdom, power, holiness, justice, and truth.'

It is worth mentioning in passing that theologians have not been alone in concocting abstract and 'unreal' schemes. The distinguished humanist philosopher F. C. S. Schiller, for example, once poked fun at the agnostic Herbert Spencer's 'Unknowable' in so far as Spencer knew far more about his 'Unknowable' than theology and revelation combined had ever been able to tell us about God!

Despite all our human limitations, we must speak about God's attributes. Indeed, I have already spoken of his faithfulness, his patience, his holy, righteous, victorious love. But I began where I believe Christians must begin: from God's revelation of himself as holy love in Christ. I do not think we can begin anywhere else—from the concept of Being, for example—and then expect to slip in what we wish to say about God-in-Christ somewhere along the way. Having begun from God's revelation we can then go on to make affirmations concerning God's nature and character, all of which will be guided by our best knowledge of him. Not indeed that God's attributes are simply descriptions which humans apply to him; he *is* his attributes, and he has made himself known as one who has certain characteristics.

I repeat that *of course* our affirmations will fall short. 'We preachers,' said Luther, 'are like young children learning to speak, and can only use half words and quarter words;' and what Luther said about preachers applies to all Christians. Again, Richard Hooker was so far correct to say that 'our safest eloquence concerning him is our silence, when we confess without confession that his glory is inexplicable, his greatness above our capacity to reach'. Luther and Hooker were but echoing Paul: 'O depth of wealth, wisdom, and knowledge in God! How unsearchable his judgements, how untraceable his ways! Who knows the mind of the Lord? Who has been his counsellor?' (Rom. 11: 33,34). As Matthew Henry said of Paul, 'Despairing to find the bottom, he humbly sits down at the

brink, and adores the depth.' But the fact that at the end we
shall find that 'praise sits silent on our tongues' (Isaac Watts)
need not inhibit us from taking up Sir Thomas Browne's
challenge to 'think magnificently about God.' As the framers of
the Congregational *Declaration of Faith* (1967) said, 'The
humility and the confidence of Christian language belong
together.' We shall be at our most confident and least arrogant
if we proceed to consider some further attributes of God in the
light of his revelation of himself as holy love in Christ.

I

The one God is self-sufficient, or independent. We depend
upon God and upon other people. God depends on no-one else.
The older theologians used to speak of God's aseity, his all-
sufficiency, his greatness; and Reformed scholars generally
spoke of his independence. God does not owe his being to
another; he requires nothing in order to make him complete. He
is the sum of all perfections, and in him there is no deficiency.

'Can man be any benefit to God?
Can even a wise man benefit him?'

Eliphaz asked these questions (Job 22: 2), and he expected the
answer, 'No.' God has character-revealing names that do not
belong to anyone else. Supreme among these is Jehovah, the one
who is what he is, and will be what he ever is (Exod. 3: 14-15).
He is the first and the last, the Alpha and the Omega (Isa. 41: 4;
Rev. 1: 8 etc.). Precisely because of his independence he is able
to give to all alike. As Paul said to the Athenians, 'It is not
because he lacks anything that he accepts service at men's
hands, for he is himself the universal giver of life and breath and
all else' (Ac. 17: 25).

It has sometimes been said that God is his own cause (*causa sui*),
but this is misleading. The doctrine of the independence of God
means that God is the *one* who is uncaused. Is he then the Absolute
of some philosophers? No, because Christians declare that the one
who is before all else is the God of holy love who makes himself
known in Christ. When Paul writes of one who 'exists before

everything, and all things are held together in him' it is of Christ as the 'image of the invisible God' of whom he speaks (Col. 1:16, 15; *cf.* Rom. 11: 36). This consideration not only 'warms up' and concretises our conception of the independent One, but it causes us to marvel more that we otherwise would that such a one, who needs nothing, should first create men for fellowship with himself, and then recreate sinners into newness of life. Grace would not seem to be quite so gracious as it is if God had been quite unable to do without the likes of us. Professor John Dickie may sum up this point for us: 'Under the influence of the scholastic, and ultimately of the Greek philosophical tradition, the old divines looked upon the absoluteness of God as part of what they learned regarding Him from the light of nature, so that in a logical point of view it came prior to their apprehension of Him in relation to mankind. But as a matter of fact to know God as absolute in the sense in which Christian theology is interested in His absoluteness is to have learned the supreme lesson of religious faith.'

It remains only to add that in talking of *one* God I have been indicating God's unity. Every day the faithful Jew recited, 'Hear, O Israel, the Lord is our God, one Lord' (Deut. 6: 4); and Christians concur. In Paul's terms, 'there is one God, the Father from whom all being comes, towards whom we move; and there is one Lord, Jesus Christ, through whom all things come to be, and we through him' (I Cor. 8: 6). If we put together the idea of God's independence and the idea of his unity we have the standing Christian reply to pantheism which, in merging God with his creation affronts his unity; and to polytheism and dualism, which deny his unity. And in asserting that there *is* such a God, and that we know him in Christ, we counter all who would try to persuade us that our God is but the projection of our own desires and wishes.

II

God is eternal and immutable. This has been implied in what I have already said. It is Isaac Watt's theme in his grand hymn of praise, 'Our God, our help in ages past':

'Before the hills in order stood,
   Or earth received her frame,
From everlasting Thou art God,
   To endless years the same.

A thousand ages in Thy sight
   Are like an evening gone;
Short as the watch that ends the night
   Before the rising sun.

Time, like an ever-rolling stream,
   Bears all its sons away;
They fly forgotten as a dream
   Dies at the opening day.'

To those words, based on *Psalm* 90, we might add these:

'My strength is broken in mid course;
   the time allotted me is short.
Snatch me not away before half my days are done,
   for thy years last through all generations.
Long ago thou didst lay the foundations of the earth,
   and the heavens were thy handiwork.
They shall pass away, but thou endurest;
   like clothes they shall all grow old;
thou shalt cast them off like a cloak,
   and they shall vanish;
but thou art the same and thy years shall have no end'
                                        (Ps. 102: 23-27).

The contrast throughout is between God's eternity and man's
brief life. God is not subject to our limitations. He is the 'I AM'.
And of Christ, who was with the Father from eternity the writer
to the Hebrews said that he is 'the same yesterday, today, and
for ever' (Heb. 13: 8). It is not that God lives longer than
anyone else; it is that he transcends time altogether: indeed,
time is his creation. Time, as Augustine said, was created *with*
the world; and in his *Address to the Greeks* Tatian declared,
'Our God did not begin to be in time; He alone is without
beginning, and He Himself is the beginning of all things.' Clock
time, with its 86,400 seconds per day, we owe to God. 'He alone
possesses immortality' (I Tim. 6: 16). If we have received eternal
life it is as a gift from God; he gives it to those who are in
Christ, his sons.

'His boundless years can ne'er decrease,
   But still maintain their prime;
Eternity's his dwelling place
   And *ever* is his time.'

                                    (I. Watts)

How eternal is God; how transient is natural man!

'Seventy years is the span of our life,
   eighty if our strength holds.'

                                  (Ps. 90: 10)

If we have any conception of the eternity of God, how apt the Preacher's words seem to be: 'God is in heaven, you are on earth; so let your words be few' (Eccles. 5: 2). The wonder is that although

'Man's days are like the grass;
   he blossoms like the flowers of the field:
a wind passes over them, and they cease to be
   and their place knows them no more'—

yet—

'the Lord's love never fails those who fear him.'
                            (Ps. 103: 15-17)

That is grace.

Now just as God's eternity indicates that he is not subject to time, so his immutability indicates that he is not subject to change. He is ever what he is, and is always true to himself (Mal. 3: 6). He can neither improve nor deteriorate. God is 'ever the same, equal and similar to himself' (Irenaeus). It does not follow from this that Christians have a static conception of God. On the contrary, he is actively present in the world; but his being is ever secure, and his nature is ever holy love. The Hebrew of the text 'I am who I am' indicates the activity of God; he is the living God (Jer. 10: 10):

'O God, the Rock of Ages,
   Who evermore hast been,
What time the tempest rages,
   Our dwelling-place serene;
Before Thy first creations,
   O Lord, the same as now,

> To endless generations
>   The Everlasting Thou.'
>
>   (Edward H. Bickersteth)

There is nothing which more readily upholds the tempest-tossed Christian than the assurance that the God who has revealed himself in Christ is the utterly reliable One, upon whom we may depend for time and for eternity:

> 'Though the mountains move and the hills shake,
>   my love shall be immovable and never fail.'
>
>   (Isa. 54: 10; *cf.* Jer. 31: 3)

'Our refuge and defence have not been from created things;' declared Stephen Charnock: 'not from the ark, but from the God of the ark. . . . In all generations he is a dwelling-place, to secure his people here, or entertain them above.' This assurance is no mere palliative; it is not an escape hatch. It is grounded upon God's self-revelation, and from our point of view it is a dire necessity. The doctrine of the immutability of God means that we are not at the mercy of caprice:

> 'My love is often low,
>   My joy still ebbs and flows;
> But peace with Him remains the same,
>   No change Jehovah knows.
>
> I change, He changes not;
>   The Christ can never die;
> His love, not mine, the resting-place;
>   His truth, not mine, the tie.'
>
>   (Horatius Bonar)

III

God is omnipresent. Just as he is unlimited by time, so God is unlimited by space which, like time, is his creation. As Solomon said in his prayer, 'Heaven itself, the highest heaven, cannot contain thee' (I Kgs. 8: 27). Again, the Psalmist rhetorically asks,

> 'Where can I escape from thy spirit?
>   Where can I flee from thy presence?

If I climb up to heaven, thou art there;
  if I make my bed in Sheol, again I find thee.
If I take my flight to the frontiers of the morning
  or dwell at the limit of the western sea,
even there thy hand will meet me
  and thy right hand will hold me fast.'

(Ps. 139: 7-10)

And Paul reminds the Athenians that God 'is not far from each one of us, for in him we live and move, in him we exist' (Ac. 17: 27-28). Of God alone it may be said that his 'centre is everywhere, His circumference nowhere' (Thomas Watson). God is unexcludable from any part of his creation: 'In no place is God's being either confined or excluded' (Augustine).

In a manner consistent with Augustine's two words some of the older theologians called God's transcendence of space his immensity, and his immanence within his creation his omnipresence. In maintaining both we have, once again, a bulwark against pantheism, and also against deism which teaches that God's power is manifested in the world whilst his essence is removed from it. Deism unacceptably keeps God at arm's length from his creation.

Some have been puzzled as to how the pure and holy God can be present in a sinful world and in the sinful heart. The Stoics had no qualms about a divine essence permeating what was base, but can a holy God of love do this? This is indeed a mystery, and it does seem that whilst man is metaphysically linked to God he can be far removed from him ethically. For all that, Thomas Watson was convinced that God's nature was not contaminated as a result of his omnipresence: 'No more than the sun shining on the dunghill is defiled, or its beauty spotted; or than Christ going among sinners was defiled, whose Godhead was a sufficient antidote against infection.' Far greater difficulties would lie in the opposite direction. If God were excluded from the heart of the sinner, what would become of the doctrine of man's creation in the image of God? Would we not be veering towards the idea of a demi-god responsible for evil, if not towards a full-blooded dualism? In Christ we have God as close to man as he could be—'yet without sin' (Heb. 4: 15).

That, for the Christian, is enough.

From the thought of God's omnipresence, and especially from the thought that he is omnipresent holy love, God's sons may draw the greatest possible comfort. 'Be we in a palace or in a cottage, in a crowd or in a corner, in a city or in a desert, in the depths of the sea or afar off upon the sea, this is certain, God is not far from everyone of us' (Matthew Henry). Because he is here he knows all about us; and that is no threat if we are sons. He is no Epicurean or deist deity, far removed from the world. The very hairs of our heads are numbered (Matt. 10: 30; Lk. 12: 7). God is close enough to hear our prayers (Ps. 65: 2); and the risen Christ is in the midst of his people as they worship (Matt. 18: 20). It has been well said that 'Omnipresence is implied in all providence, in all prayer, all communion with God and reliance upon God' (W. N. Clarke). Let us be taught by the evangelist Brownlow North, who brings out the consequences of omnipresent holy love:

> 'God is always present with us. To realize this, to believe it, and to act as if it were a truth, is what we should seek for before all things. That it is so, is our only safety. "In Thy presence is fulness of joy." This is simple truth. Let us ask ourselves if we would and do feel it joy to be in the Lord's presence. To many the very idea of being in God's presence is horror of horrors. This is because they are unconverted. Never rest till you are enabled to desire God's presence, and to rejoice in it.'

IV

God is omniscient. Here we have the great claim that the holy God, who alone knows himself as he truly is, knows everything else as well. There are no limits to his knowledge. He knows everything that he has made: the stars (Ps. 147: 4); the sparrows (Matt. 10: 29); and men (Ps. 33: 13-15). Since he is eternal, he knows all things from eternity (Ac. 15: 18). He knows past, present and future; he sees the end from the beginning. It seems to me that in speaking of God's omniscience we are face to face with an insoluble puzzle, and with a practical reality.

First, the puzzle. It concerns God's foreknowledge: his

knowledge of things yet to be. For his part Aristotle denied that future events could with certainty be known; and Socinus stimulated a train of thought which led some to the view that God could not foreknow the acts of free men, since if *God* the infallible One knew what men would in fact do, men would in fact do those things, and would not, therefore, be free. The Unitarian Martineau denied that God knew whether or not Martineau would yield to temptation at midday. In a word the puzzle concerns God's omniscience which, it would seem, must include his foreknowledge, and man's freedom to act or not to act.

It may help a little if we remember that since God is eternal, he sees past, present and future in an eternal NOW: 'with the Lord one day is like a thousand years and a thousand years like one day' (II Pet. 3: 8; *cf*. Ps. 90: 4). Strictly speaking, then, the 'fore' in 'foreknowledge' can apply only within our time-conditioned experience. If we speak of God's foreknowledge at all, we must realise that we are drawing an analogy from our experience, and that this analogy, while it enables us to avoid utter silence, does not entirely encompass its object.

It may further help if we see that those who deny God's omniscience in the interests of man's freedom are on the way to leaving us with a free-wheeling universe. Such a universe needs no god. We must hold that the all-knowing God in no way compromises man's relative freedom. (I say 'relative' freedom because man can only be free in ways appropriate to man; he is not free to fly, for example. Similarly with God: he cannot be ungodlike; he cannot sin; he cannot act against his nature by rewarding evil-doers, telling lies, acting inconstantly, and so on). To say that God foreknows is not to say that he denies genuine freedom to man. As Stephen Charnock long ago saw:

> 'That God doth foreknow everything, and yet that there is liberty in the rational creature, are both certain; but how fully to reconcile them, may surmount the understanding of man.'

The practical reality is that the believer is confronted by the Fatherly God of holy love, who knows all about him. The fact that God knows all about us and our needs gives us no reason to cease to pray to him. Prayer is a means of expressing our fellowship with him, and of seeking to bring our desires into line with his will. In any case, there is far more to prayer than informing God of our needs: there is adoration, confession, intercession, thanksgiving:

> 'Prayer was not appointed for God's information as if he were ignorant, but for the expression of our desires; not to furnish him with a knowledge of what we want [i.e. lack], but to manifest to him by some rational sign convenient to our nature, our sense of that want, which he knows by himself.'
>
> (S. Charnock)

But more than that: we only truly know ourselves when we are known by God. This was the point emphasised by James Denney in one of his sermons. The Psalmist was not speculating upon an abstract concept of God's omniscience when he said, 'Lord, thou hast examined me and knowest me' (Ps. 139: 1). Said Denney,

> 'The Psalmist is as certain of God as he is of his own existence; indeed it is not too much to say that it is only as he is conscious of being searched and known by God— only as he is overwhelmed by contact with a spirit which knows him better than he knows himself—that he rises to any adequate sense of what his own being and personality mean. He is revealed to himself by God's search; he knows himself through God.'

According to the nature of our 'walk' the thought of the all-knowing God consoles us or convicts us. No doubt an unhealthy concentration upon the all-knowing God (Prov. 15: 3; *cf.* 5: 21; Job: 31: 4; 34: 21,22) can, as J. B. Phillips realised, lead to the unfortunate view of God as a resident policeman, ever poised to pounce upon us when we fall. This is a most unhappy view of God (not to mention the police!) But the possibility of thinking of him in this way only serves to underline the importance of thinking of the attributes of God *together*. They qualify one another. The omniscient One is the holy loving Father who is absolutely straight with his sons. Certainly a modicum of godly fear does not come amiss! When men say,

> 'The Lord does not see,
>   The God of Jacob pays no heed,'

they need to be asked,

> 'Shall not he that instructs the nations correct them?
>   The teacher of mankind, has he no knowledge?'
>   (Ps. 94: 7,9,10)

John Newton attempts to express the way in which omniscience both consoles and convicts in this hymn:

> 'Great God! from Thee there's nought concealed,
>   Thou seest my inward frame;
> To Thee I always stand revealed
>   Exactly as I am!
>
> Since I can hardly, therefore, bear
>   What in myself I see;
> How vile and black I must appear,
>   Most holy God, to Thee!
>
> But since my Saviour stands between,
>   In garments dyed in blood,
> 'Tis He, instead of me is seen,
>   When I approach to God.
>
> Thus, though a sinner, I am safe;
>   He pleads, before the throne,
> His life and death in my behalf,
>   And calls my sins His own.
>
> What wondrous love, what mysteries,
>   In this appointment shine!
> My breaches of the law are His,
>   And His obedience mine.'

It remains only to add that the wisdom of God has been much discussed by theologians down the ages. A knowledgeable person is not always wise; but God is infinitely wise. He is all-discerning. He *wisely* renders his knowledge practicable. His wisdom is his divine skill in appointing the means for the realisation of his purposes. He makes no blunders. What a comfort this is!

> 'God shall alone my refuge be,
>   And comfort of my mind;

Too wise to be mistaken, He,
Too good to be unkind.'

(Samuel Medley)

'The patience of God would be cowardice, his power an oppression, his justice a tyranny, without wisdom as the spring, and holiness as the rule' (S. Charnock). He is wise in creation; wise in providence; and wise in his ultimate purpose. These are the themes of the next three chapters. I promise something on the final 'o', omnipotence, in the last chapter. Meanwhile, let us reflect upon the one, self-sufficient, eternal, unchangeable, omnipresent, omniscient, wise God of holy love, of whom John Mason sang,

'How great a being, Lord, is Thine,
    Which doth all beings keep!
Thy knowledge is the only line
    To sound so vast a deep.
Thou art a sea without a shore,
    A sun without a sphere;
Thy time is now and evermore,
    Thy place is everywhere.'

* * * * *

A Hymn:

'O God, Thou bottomless abyss!
    Thee to perfection who can know?
O height immense! What words suffice
    Thy countless attributes to show?

Unfathomable depths Thou art;
    O plunge me in Thy mercy's sea!
Void of true wisdom is my heart;
    With love embrace and cover me.

Eternity Thy fountain was,
    Which, like Thee, no beginning knew;
Thou wast ere time began his race,
    Ere glowed with stars the ethereal blue.

Greatness unspeakable is Thine,
    Greatness, whose undiminished ray,
When short-lived worlds are lost, shall shine,
    When earth and heaven are fled away.

Unchangeable, all-perfect Lord,
    Essential life's unbounded sea,

What lives and moves, lives by Thy word;
    It lives, and moves, and is from Thee.

High is Thy power above all height,
    Whate'er Thy will decrees is done;
Thy wisdom, equal to Thy might
      Only to Thee, O God, is known.'
                      (Ernst Lange; *tr.* John Wesley)

A Prayer:

Holy God, all-perfect One, receive us who are blemished;
Holy God, unlimited One, save us who are confined;
Holy God, all-knowing One, illumine us who are confused;
Holy God, all-wise One, teach us discernment,
And lead us in the way everlasting. Through Jesus Christ, our Lord, AMEN.

5

The Great Original

Augustine has a story of a good old man who was asked what God did before the world was created. 'He made a hell for the inquisitive,' the old man replied. Leaving on one side the perfectly proper objection that we cannot speak of a time *before* creation since time was created *with* creation, I wish to point out that there are ways of being inquisitive about creation which miss most of the points which the *Christian* doctrine of creation is concerned to make. I shall set down five bald statements, and then devote a section to each:

1. Christians need the Christian doctrine of creation.
2. The Christian doctrine of creation cannot conflict with natural science.
3. The Christian doctrine of creation underlines the truth concerning God's sovereignty, and stands as a bulwark against alien creation theories and inadequate views of God.
4. The Christian doctrine of creation is inextricably interwoven with the Christian doctrine of redemption, re-creation.
5. The Christian doctrine of creation is thoroughly practical in that it prompts our worship and has implications for our conduct.

I

Christians need the Christian doctrine of creation. In the five statements I have just made, and in this repetition of the first, I reiterate, almost to the point of boredom, the phrase, 'The

Christian doctrine of creation.' This is because of my profound conviction that there is a truly distinctive Christian doctrine of creation which differs from all other creation doctrines, ancient or modern. The Christian doctrine attributes the origin of all things to the God we know in Christ—the God of holy, Fatherly love. He and no other is the creator. Indeed, the Christian doctrine goes further than that. You will notice that I have not spoken of the *biblical* doctrine of creation. This is not because the Christian doctrine is not biblical, or unbiblical; it is because I wish to caution us against allowing our minds to fly too quickly and too exclusively to the first two chapters of Genesis, or to Psalm 104—magnificent as they are.

As I see it the *Christian* doctrine of creation is affirmed in such a verse as this: 'The Word, then, was with God from the beginning, and through him all things came to be; no single thing was created without him' (Jn. 1: 2,3). Here we have the stupendous claim that Christ, the Word made flesh is he who, as eternal Son, was actively involved with the Father from the beginning. Christians read all the rest of the biblical material on creation in the light of that conviction.

Although the doctrine of creation is, from every point of view, a foundation doctrine, it is not the first fully to be set forth. This is true whether we consider the Old Testament or the New. Perhaps the high point of Old Testament thought on the creator-God is this:

'Thus says the Lord, the creator of the heavens,
　he who is God,
who made the earth and fashioned it
　and himself fixed it fast,
who created it no empty void,
　but made it for a place to dwell in:
I am the Lord, there is no other.'

(Isa. 45: 18)

But this was a conviction which the prophet reached after reflecting upon the way in which God had led his people through history. He had saved them from Egypt; he had borne with them in their sin; he had appointed kings to rule them and prophets to declare his word to them; and even though they were now exiled in Babylon, he would one day restore them to their own land. From this idea that history is the theatre of the activity of God there flowed the idea that he who is in control of history is he who made history's stage.

Similarly in the New Testament: the disciples followed Jesus; they heard his words, they saw his deeds; they did not fully understand him at first. After Peter's confession of faith at Caesarea Philippi (Matt. 16: 16; Mk. 8: 29; Lk. 9: 20) Jesus resolutely set his face to go to Jerusalem, there to face his Cross, there to win his Resurrection. Increasingly the conviction deepened that he whose ministry had been so wonderful, and whose triumph so astounding, could be none other than the Lord of history. He was *the* Son of the Father, who had been with the Father from all eternity. As with the disciples, so with us: 'We become aware of One Whom Jesus persuades us to call "God the Father", and we go on to recognise that He must be Creator of all things. Then, and only then, do we *know* that God exists, and what it means to say that He is the Creator. And all this we have learnt, not from the study of Nature, but from the revelation of "God the Father"' (W. A. Whitehouse).

The celebrated preacher, C. H. Spurgeon, put it like this: 'The old saying is "Go from Nature up to Nature's God." But it is hard work going up hill. The best thing is to go from Nature's God down to Nature; and, if you once get to Nature's God and believe him and love him, it is surprising how easy it is to hear music in the waves, and songs in the wild whisperings of the winds, and to see God everywhere.' (This is consistent with what I said in the first chapter about the design argument for the existence of God).

We must always begin with the God we know because he has made himself known in Christ. 'You say that Design never leads to the Infinite,' said 'Rabbi' Duncan to a friend, 'and it never yields the idea of creation. I would add that it never gives one the Infinite *because* it never gives me creation.' *Of course* it requires an act of faith to begin from God-in-Christ: 'By faith we perceive that the world was fashioned by the word of God' (Heb. 11: 3); but there is no other way. This has been granted not only by Christians, but also by the non-Christian philosopher

Professor A. G. N. Flew who, at the end of a discussion of creation, said, 'The heart of the matter is that the only satisfactory and perhaps the sufficient justification for the whole enterprise of trying to say things which it seems necessarily cannot be said lies just there; in Christ. "In the riddle of a life lived and a death died."' What a wealth of meaning Christians can put into the words of Philo, the Alexandrian Jew: 'Whilst the human voice is made to be heard, God's voice is made to be seen.'

As we look back across the biblical testimony with Christian eyes we can catch something of the grandeur of the first two chapters of Genesis. We can see too how different in tone they are from the creation sagas of other lands, with which they have often been compared. The great theme of Genesis 2: 4-25 is that man, the crown of creation, is utterly dependent upon God, and that he owes absolute obedience to God. The theme of Genesis 1: 1-2: 3 (the later, Priestly account) is that man, the crown of creation, is God's steward; he has dominion over all else that God has created.

The biblical creation is *good*. There is no notion here that matter is evil, or that it owes its origin to an inferior or subordinate god; there is no suggestion that matter is an eternal principle opposed to God—such are two dualist positions. But although creation is good, it is not God, as pantheism holds. The heavens do declare God's glory (Ps. 19: 1), but he is their originator. Again, whereas in the Babylonian creation myth God is light, in Genesis God *creates* light; and where Babylonian myths have the supreme deity emerging from a host of lesser, squabbling deities, in Genesis God is absolutely original. He emerges from nothing; he creates all things.

But we do not only look backward with Christian eyes, we look forward too. The Christ who is the Word of creation is the Lord of heaven and earth (Rev. 4). He is the judge of heaven and earth (Rev. 5), and the re-creator of a new heaven and a new earth (Rev. 21). For the Christian creation is an unexcludable doctrine.

In my opening statement I said that Christians *need* this doctrine. Now this might appear to be so obvious that it does

not need to be said. In fact, however, some Christians do not
give very much thought to the doctrine of creation. They so
immerse themselves in the practice of Christian worship, in the
nurturing of their sacramental life, or in Christian busyness of
one kind or another, that serious thought about most Christian
doctrines, but especially about the creation doctrine, is crowded
out. Or, they so dwell upon the fact that in Christ God has
saved them into newness of life that they find the doctrine of
creation somewhat tame, or, at least, remote. They have not
seen that 'He is appointed the author of our bliss who was the
author of our being' (Matthew Henry). Some Christians may
half fear that if they do think about this doctrine, and if they
dare to discuss it with their scientifically-minded friends, they
may very soon be out of their depth.

But all the great certainties of the Christian faith, and all the
grounds of the Christian's hope turn upon the Christian
doctrine of creation. Here is James Orr's classic statement of the
matter:

> 'To feel that we and our world, that our human life and all
> that we are and have, absolutely depend on God,—this is
> the primary attitude of religion. For if they do not thus
> depend,—if there is anything in the universe which exists
> out of and independently of God,—then what guarantee
> have we for the unfailing execution of His purposes, what
> ground have we for that assured trust in His Providence
> which Christ inculcates, what security have we that all
> things will work together for good? But to affirm that all
> things depend on God is just another way to affirm the
> creation of all things by God. They would not depend on
> Him if He were not their Creator. They do depend on
> Him, because they are created by Him. The doctrine of
> creation, therefore, is not a mere speculation. Only this
> conviction that it is "the Lord that made heaven and
> earth"—that "of Him, and through Him, and to Him, are
> all things"—that He has created all things, and for His
> pleasure they are and were created,—can give us the
> confidence we need in a holy and wise government of the
> universe, and in a final triumph of good over evil.'

II

The Christian doctrine of creation cannot conflict with

natural science. I have put this baldly in the negative because many have found it necessary to *assert* conflict equally baldly! As everybody knows, natural scientists have made one discovery after another; the explosion of knowledge has been phenomenal; and as a result, 'science' has gained considerable psychological advantage. So there lingers in many minds the notion that scientists can tell us what the truth is, what the facts are (though in many areas many scientists themselves are not so sure), and that the Christian perversely closes his mind against hard evidence whilst consoling himself with legends and autosuggestion.

Some Christians, anxious to maintain their position, have made strenuous efforts to show that the discoveries of science do not conflict with the Genesis creation narratives. They have made much of the fact that the Hebrew for the 'days' of creation can indicate lengthy periods of time, and they have concluded that once this is seen the requirements of the geologist and the astronomer can be accommodated.

I do not find it necessary to look for such compatibilities, for I hold that the Christian doctrine is not affected in any way by scientific findings as to the when or the how of creation. This is not to say that the Christian ought not to be grateful for all that science reveals concerning God's handiwork; it is only to say that it is not for science as such to say whether or not it is *God's* handiwork. Again, I am not suggesting that the subject matters of science, broadly conceived, and Christianity do not overlap. They do, and it could not be otherwise. For on the one hand the Christian faith is bound up with history, with the material world, with a revelation in the *flesh*; and on the other hand modern science owes more than some of its practitioners are prepared to admit to the Christian faith. The motivation of many scientists of an earlier day (and of some in our own time) was that they were engaged in something like an act of worship: they were co-operating with the creator as the creator progressively revealed his hand; and they regarded themselves as assuming the constancy of God's created order every time they made an experiment. The fact remains, however, that if, after doing his work the scientist declares, 'There is a creator,' or 'There is not a creator,' he, no less than the Christian, is making an affirmation of faith.

The Christian sings,

> 'The spacious firmament on high,
> With all the blue ethereal sky,
> And spangled heavens, a shining frame,
> Their great Original proclaim . . .'

(Joseph Addison)

The scientist who is a Christian may sing it too; but he could not use his science to prove or to disprove it. Science deals with causal relationships within the natural order, and that is precisely what the doctrine of *creation* is not about.

Against this background I can draw the sting of the hypothesis of evolution. Some Christians still regard evolution as posing a grave threat to the faith, whilst others have all too eagerly swallowed the doctrine. The truth is that the idea of evolution works most successfully in its original home, biology. There had, of course, been notions of progress and development long before Darwin—in fact, way back in classical Greece. What Darwin did was to provide evidence to show the process by which evolution occurred. This was the process of natural selection—what Herbert Spencer was to call the principle of 'the survival of the fittest.' But even if it could be shown that the idea of evolution is not only problem-free in biology, but universally applicable, it still could not answer the question, 'Why is there anything at all?' Evolution presupposes the existence of something that evolves; it does not tell us the origin of that something. So I think that there is much to be said for the opinion of the Methodist Samuel Chadwick that 'Evolution is neither proved by science nor denied by scripture.'

Above all, evolution cannot give an adequate account of the nature of man. Hence the modified versions of the evolutionary theory which allow for 'stages'. But to admit stages is to sell the pass to those who have other ways of accounting for man's uniqueness among created things. In olden time it was put thus: 'the Lord God formed a man from the dust of the ground and breathed into his nostrils the breath of life. Thus man became a living creature' (Gen. 2: 7). It was God's doing.

Before leaving the specifically scientific realm I would mention in passing the Steady State hypothesis and the Explosion, or Big Bang, theories of the creation of the universe. According to the former theory galaxies come and go, and creation is continuous; according to the latter, the universe 'arrived' out of a void. But in either case the question 'Why?' may be asked, and science as such is at a loss to answer. The Christian, taking his courage in both hands, declares, 'However and whenever creation occurred, it was at the express will of the Fatherly God of holy love;' and his reason for saying this has more to do with Easter than with natural science:

> 'Yes, God is good, all nature says,
>   By God's own hand with speech endued;
> And man, in louder notes of praise,
>   Should sing for joy that God is good.
>
> For all Thy gifts we bless Thee, Lord;
>   But most for Thy redeeming blood,
> Thy pardoning grace, Thy quickening word,
>   These prompt our songs that God is good.'
>
> (John H. Gurney)

III

The Christian doctrine of creation underlines the truth concerning God's sovereignty, and stands as a bulwark against alien creation theories and inadequate views of God. The Bible is in no doubt as to God's sovereignty in creation:

> 'For he spoke, and it was;
>   he commanded, and it stood firm.'
>
> (Ps. 33: 9)

One of the traditional ways of making this point has been to speak of creation out of nothing (*ex nihilo*). This doctrine is not taught in so many words in the Bible, though many scholars believe that it is clearly implicit there. We find what is perhaps the earliest explicit reference to the idea in the Apocrypha, where the mother of the Maccabees says, 'I beg you, child, look at the sky and the earth; see all that is in them and realize that

God made them out of nothing, and that man comes into being in the same way' (II Macc. 7: 28).

It goes without saying that the doctrine of creation *ex nihilo* does not mean that God made the universe out of a lot of 'stuff' called 'nothing'. Rather, it means that the universe was not *made* out of anything. Creation is an utterly original act of God: matter and time together. This was the view of Augustine and Irenaeus, and it would seem that the authors of the Apostles' Creed intended their opening sentence to be taken in the same way: 'I believe in God the Father almighty, Maker of heaven and earth . . .' They did not think of God's making something out of already existing materials, as I might make a tea tray out of wood; they thought of an absolutely original act. They would not have accepted the view of the nineteenth-century Unitarian Martineau, who maintained that God had space to work with. On the contrary, God had nothing to work with, and he created all things. Again, creation *ex nihilo* does not mean that the universe is uncaused; it is an affirmation that God's will is its cause.

By the time of the Apocryphal books the influence of Greek thought was increasing, so that alongside the Maccabees statement we may place a verse from the Wisdom of Solomon which speaks of 'thy almighty hand, which created the world out of formless matter . . .' (11: 17). The implication here is that the formless matter was *there* from eternity, and that what God did was to shape it into the world we know. This doctrine, espoused by Plato, did not become standard within Christianity, though Justin Martyr did not reject it outright. What the early Fathers did unanimously reject was any suggestion of polytheism. We do not owe the world to a number of gods—least of all to a number of squabbling, rival gods. The world is the handiwork of the one sovereign Lord. Nor is it simply that one God made it and not many; it is that there are no others; all other so-called gods are impostors. Here we are firmly back upon the Hebrew track once more. One of the most delightfully ironic attacks upon false gods comes from the unknown prophet of the Babylonian exile, the author of Isaiah 40-55. He mocks those who use wood in so many ways and then make a god out of the *residue*:

'A man plants a cedar and the rain makes it grow, so that
later on he will have cedars to cut down; or he chooses an
ilex or an oak to raise a stout tree for himself in the forest.
It becomes fuel for his fire: some of it he takes and warms
himself, some he kindles and bakes bread on it, and some
he makes into a god and prostrates himself, shaping it into
an idol and bowing down before it. The one half of it he
burns in the fire and on this he roasts meat, so that he may
eat his roast and be satisfied; he also warms himself at it
and he says, "Good! I can feel the heat, I am growing
warm." Then what is left of the wood he makes into a god
by carving it into shape; he bows down to it and
prostrates himself and prays to it, saying, "Save me; for
thou art my god."'

(Isa. 44: 14-17)

The same writer scorns the 'gods' who, far from saving their
people, are carried off into captivity:

'Bel has crouched down, Nebo has stooped low:
    their images, once carried in your processions,
have been loaded on to beasts and cattle,
    a burden for the weary creatures;
they stoop and they crouch;
    not for them to bring the burden to safety;
the gods themselves go into captivity.'

(Isa. 46: 1,2)

The prophet puts his positive point thus:

'I am the Lord, there is no other;
    I make the light, I create darkness . . .'
        (Isa. 45: 6-7; *cf.* 40: 12; Jer. 32: 17; Amos 4: 19)

And the psalmist agrees:

'For the gods of the nations are idols every one;
    but the Lord made the heavens.'

(Ps. 96: 5)

In the early days of the Church some, especially the Syrian
Gnostics, were teaching that the world was an emanation from
God, rather than a distinct creation of his. Origen agreed that
creation was eternal, but denied that the world was an
emanation; on the contrary, he held that there was a time when
God existed but the world did not. When we come to the

Reformation we find Calvin declaring that 'to think of God as a Creator only for a moment . . . were frigid and jejune . . .' In other words, God, having created the world, does not then leave it to its own devices, as some of the eighteenth-century Deists thought. He is ever creatively active.

Let me now attempt a summary statement: creation is *ex nihilo*. It is the free work of the sovereign God of holy love whom we know in Christ. It did not involve the shaping of already existing materials; it is not a question of emanation, or of team-work. Although independent of God the universe depends upon God for its continuance in being, and he continues to superintend it in creative ways as he works towards the final manifestation of his glory. Paul put much of it in this way: 'In him [i.e. the Son] everything in heaven and on earth was created, not only things visible but also the invisible orders of thrones, sovereignties, authorities and powers: the whole universe has been created through him and for him. And he exists before everything, and all things are held together in him' (Col. 1: 16,17).

Christian thinkers of the ages echo the same idea. Speaking of God Augustine says that 'It is His occult power which pervades all things . . . which gives being to all that is, and modifies and limits its existence so that without Him it would not be thus, and would not have any being at all.' Aquinas concurs: 'It must be said that every being in any way existing is from God.' And in one of the most popular of traditional Christmas carols, 'The First Nowel', we sing of him, 'That hath made heaven and earth of nought . . .'.

I have already hinted at some of the ways in which the Christian doctrine of creation steers a course between alien doctrinal rocks. These rocks are so important and hazardous that I must briefly specify them by way of warning.

The Christian doctrine of creation opposes:

1. *Pantheism*. Pantheism merges God with the phenomenal world. 'All is God' says the pantheist. Christians hold that God, though creatively present within the universe, transcends it—certainly the creation is not an emanation from him as the Syrian Gnostics and Swedenborg held. Only by

countering pantheism can our understanding of God remain fully personal; only so can it remain moral—for what price a god who is as readily identified with evil as with good?

2. *Deism*. Deism teaches that God, having created the world, left it to its own devices, rather as one might wind up a clock and leave it to run. This view makes for God's remoteness, and he might as well be as impersonal as the god of pantheism. It leads to a static notion of God, whereas the Bible represents God as being continuously active (Jn. 5: 17).

3. *Polytheism*. Against the view that there are many gods Christianity maintains that there is one God only, and that he has made himself known as Creator-Saviour in Christ.

4. *Dualism*. There have been many dualistic theories in the course of human history. In some God, as the principle of order, is opposed to chaos; in others he is set over against matter which is hostile to him. We find versions of this latter theory in the writings of the Gnostics Basilides and Valentinus, and in the teaching of Hinduism; and in the nineteenth century John Stuart Mill thought of God as being hindered by the intractable nature of the materials at his disposal. Christians cannot hold that matter is evil, for 'God saw all that he had made, and it was very good' (Gen. 1: 31). I do not minimise the harrowing importance of the presence of evil in the world, and I shall have more to say about it in the next chapter. Suffice it for the present to say that Christians cannot seek a solution to the problem in any kind of dualism.

5. *Maya*. In view of all that I have said I need only briefly make plain that Christianity cannot believe that the created world and the history of man are *maya*, illusion. This eastern doctrine cannot in any way be squared with the idea of a God who sends his Son into the world; whose Son dies upon the Cross and is raised; whose Son inaugurates a Church, a community with a purpose, in the world, and so on. The Christian God is one who does not shun the real world as it is. On the contrary, he gives himself for it.

Two points remain to be made. First, there is a sense in which God, being ever what he is, must be eternally creator—just as he is eternally Father. But this is not to say that he was under the necessity of creating in order to be God. Rather, he willed to create because he is love, and because he desired fellowship with men. As a prominent Danish theologian of the nineteenth century said,

> 'In a certain sense one may say that God created the world in order to satisfy a want [i.e. lack] in Himself; but the idea of God's love requires us to understand this want as quite as truly a *superfluity*. For this lack in God is not, as in the God of Pantheism, a blind hunger and thirst after existence, but is identical with the inexhaustible riches of that liberty which cannot but will to reveal itself.'
>
> (Martensen)

Again, 'God creates, not to supply his own need out of what is beyond himself, but rather from pure love of creation and out of the riches of his own eternal being' (O. C. Quick). God is, as Jonathan Edwards saw, *disposed* to communicate his fulness to others.

The second point concerns the word 'liberty' which Martensen used—or 'free' which I used when I said that creation is 'the free work of the sovereign God of holy love whom we know in Christ.' My intention was to underline the fact that no one does or could stand over God; nor does the universe proceed, as Spinoza thought, by logical necessity from an absolute substance, or, as Hegel thought, from an impersonal Reason. Creation is the free act of a personal God. If he creates it is because he wills to do so: 'Thou didst create all things; by thy will they were created, and have their being!' (Rev. 4: 11). God is *sovereign*. But *God* is sovereign; and God is the holy God of Fatherly love. Whatever he does is done in love. Creation, then, must in some sense be an act of his grace. Let us explore this idea further.

IV

The Christian doctrine of creation is inextricably interwoven with the Christian doctrine of redemption, re-creation. 'The conversion of a sinner.' said the Puritan John Mason, 'is a greater wonder than the creation of the world.' Or, in the words of Mason's contemporary Charnock,

'It is more skill to make a curious piece of workmanship with ill-conditioned tools, than with instruments naturally fitted for the work. It is no such great wonder for a limner to draw an exact piece with a fit pencil and suitable colours, as to begin and perfect a beautiful work with a straw and water, things improper for such a design. This wisdom of God is more admirable and astonishing, than if a man were able to rear a vast palace by fire, whose nature is to consume combustible matter, not to erect a building.'

These words help us to keep things in perspective. They remind us that God, having created the world, has not thereby exhausted his powers. It will not do to say that 'in creation God shows His hand, but in redemption He shows His heart,' for this is to divide God's works. Both creation and redemption are works of his love. In face of man's sin and alienation the creator God proceeds with his gracious work of re-creation, ever working out his purpose until there appears that 'new heaven and new earth' of which the exiled John had a vision on the island of Patmos (Rev. 21: 1).

Christians, therefore, are right to sing,

> 'Great God of wonders, all Thy ways
>   Are matchless, godlike, and divine;
> But the fair glories of Thy grace
>   More godlike and unrivalled shine.'
>   (Samuel Davies)

But they should at the same time remember that the 'grace' in the third line is 'saving grace'. There as nowhere else we see God's inexhaustible love; yet this is not to deny that all God's works are expressions of his Fatherly love. For 'the divine purpose which is now apprehended as at work within the world through Christ "soul-saving", must have originally made the world so that in its essential constitution it was suitable to "soul-making"' (H. H. Farmer). Or, as Dr Whitehouse put it, 'God is preserving a creation which does not bring to him the credit he deserves . . . The Lord who rules it is the Lord who was crucified within it.' But he was not only crucified, he was raised. Hence the new creation is assured. The Church, the people of God, is the earnest of, and the witness to, God's re-creation.

The atheist philosopher Marcuse has seen the need of 'a new type of man . . . capable of finding a qualitatively different kind of life . . .' Christianity knows the same need, but knows too that the qualitatively different kind of life is a gift to be received; and it knows whence that gift comes. It comes from the God who graciously intervenes; and as John Huxtable said, 'The divine invader is the original designer.' Hence our guarantee that the grace offered in Christ is sovereign grace:

> 'His very word of grace is strong
>   As that which built the skies:
> The voice that rolls the stars along
>   Speaks all the promises.'

(Isaac Watts)

Hence too the Christian's prayer:

> 'That was a wonder-working word,
>   Which could the vast creation raise;
> Angels attendant on their Lord,
>   Admired the plan, and sung His praise.
>
> But man, the lord and crown of all,
>   By sin his honour soon defaced;
> His heart (How altered since the fall!)
>   Is dark, deformed, and void, and waste.
>
> The new creation of the soul
>   Does now no less His power display.
> Than when He formed the mighty whole,
>   And kindled darkness into day.
>
> Though self-destroyed, O Lord, we are,
>   Yet let us feel what Thou canst do;
> Thy word the ruin can repair,
>   And all our hearts create anew.'

(John Newton)

V

The Christian doctrine of creation is thoroughly practical in that it prompts our worship and has implications for our conduct.

1. It prompts our worship:

> 'God the Creator,
>   Mighty Creator,
> Sovereign of air, sea and land;
>   Rugged crag and tiny flower,
> Show Thy wisdom and Thy power,
>   And we too are the work of Thy hand.'

So sings the contemporary hymn writer Ken Battye in authentic Christian tones.

The celebrated entomologist, Fabre, was once asked whether or not he believed in God. 'No,' he replied. 'I don't *believe* in God; I *see* him everywhere.' Nature is wonderful, and worship of nature's creator is entirely appropriate. But nature is not God, so nature must not be worshipped, nor must any created thing: 'You shall have no other god to set against me. You shall not make a carved image for yourself... You shall not bow down to them or worship them...' (Exod. 20: 3-5). Why? Because 'I am the Lord who brought you out of Egypt, out of the land of slavery' (Exod. 20: 2). Is there any other such Saviour? No! Then worship him alone. The true Christian no less than the faithful Hebrew knows that 'thou art worthy, O Lord our God, to receive glory and honour and power, because thou didst create all things' (Rev. 4: 11). And Paul reminded the Romans in no uncertain terms that at the heart of the sin of the wicked was the fact that they had 'offered reverence and worship to created things instead of to the Creator' (Rom. 1: 25). It may not be inappropriate in this chapter to point out that science can be an idol, so can philosophy, so can any 'ism'.

2. The Christian doctrine of creation has implications for our conduct. In a nutshell the point is that we are accountable stewards. We are placed in God's creation by God, for God. We can exploit the material universe to good ends or bad. The way we use our bodies and spend our time and nurture our gifts can glorify our creator—or not. So can the way we spend our money and use the earth's scarce resources—as individuals and as nations. I can think of no practical matter of Christian living which is not made clearer and more challenging by being

reviewed in the light of the Christian doctrine of creation. In all such cases the words, 'it is he that hath made us, and we are his own' (Ps. 100:3) positively ring in our ears.

Never before has this truth come home to man with such ominous portent. With every new scientific advance fresh ethical challenges are presented. One example, quoted by Professor Whitehouse from a British Council of Churches report on *The Era of Atomic Power* will make the point clearly enough:

'There is a difference of worlds between man seeking to know the wonders of God's creation, and man exploring without reverence the secrets of a universe from which God, binding law, and moral obligation, have all been removed. It is when the transition takes place from man as a searcher for truth to man as the self-sufficient controller of Nature, that what he discovers is turned to misuse, and is even falsified in respect of its own significance.'

The Christian doctrine of creation reminds us that although God is distinct from his creation, he is not removed from it. It is his, and it is the theatre of his activity. Man may not, therefore, do as he likes with it. He has the high privilege of being God's under-steward, but he dare not treat the material creation as so much disposable property, or other people or himself as objects. Without reverence the technician exploits; without stewardship the mystic retreats. Wondering contemplation of the creation doctrine should prompt not desecration, but consecration:

'Almighty Father of all things that be,
 Our life, our work, we consecrate to Thee,
Whose heavens declare Thy glory from above,
 Whose earth below is witness to Thy love.'
(Ernest Edward Dugmore)

Such consecration can only be offered by the grateful heart, and since creation and the new creation belong together, 'what one looks for in the world is anything which evokes in Christian men a gratitude which is all of a piece with the gratitude of the believer for the grace of his Lord Jesus Christ' (W. A. Whitehouse).

* * * * *

A Hymn:

> 'Nature with open volume stands,
>   To spread her maker's praise abroad,
> And every labour of his hands,
>   Shows something worthy of a God.
>
> But in the grace that rescued man,
>   His brightest form of glory shines;
> Here, on the cross, 'tis fairest drawn
>   In precious blood, and crimson lines.
>
> Here His whole Name appears complete:
>   Nor wit can guess, nor reason prove,
> Which of the letters best is writ,
>   The power, the wisdom, or the love.
>
> O the sweet wonders of that cross
>   Where Christ my Saviour loved, and died!
> Her noblest life my spirit draws
>   From His dear wounds, and bleeding side.
>
> I would for ever speak His Name
>   In sounds to mortal ears unknown,
> With angels join to praise the Lamb,
>   And worship at His Father's throne.'

(Isaac Watts)

A Prayer that we may be enabled to see the creator in his creation:

> 'Thou who hast given me eyes to see
>   And love this sight so fair,
> Give me a heart to find out Thee,
>   And read Thee everywhere.'

(John Keble)

A Prayer for personal re-creation:

'Lord! thou hast once made me, make me anew; sin has defaced thy image in me, oh draw it again by the pencil of the Holy Ghost.'

(Thomas Watson)

6

Thy Providence Is Kind and Large

The programme for a performance of Handel's *Messiah* contained a printer's error. One letter only was involved, but what a difference it made! The line in the Hallelujah Chorus now read, 'Hallelujah, for the Lord God omnipotent *resigneth*.' The doctrine of providence teaches that God *never* resigns. 'It were cold and lifeless,' said Calvin, 'to represent God as a momentary Creator, who completed his work once for all, and then left it.' On the contrary, 'God is not like an artificer that builds a house, and then leaves it, but like a pilot he steers the ship of the whole creation' (Thomas Watson). 'Providence,' declared Richard Sibbes, 'is the perpetuity and continuance of creation;' and John Mason affirmed that 'without God's providence nothing falls out in the world; without His commission, nothing stirs; without His blessing, nothing prospers'.

But what the older Puritan writers did not always make clear was that the providence of God is the providence of the Fatherly God of holy love whom we know in Christ. True to the scholastic tradition, they held that quite apart from revelation the providence of God could rationally be demonstrated from the natural order; one had only to look and reflect in order to see the plan and divine the purpose. A harder rationalism, and rival theories—not to mention the calamities of our century, have taught us otherwise. The Danish theologian Martensen was among those who early grasped the point. 'Human history,' he wrote, 'finds its *centre*, its true meaning, in the revelation of

Jesus Christ. It is only in the light which comes from him that
humanity can look back upon a past which is full of meaning,
can look forward to a future full of promise, and can
contemplate its development as an organic whole.'

Christians know God as he has made himself known
in Christ. When we think of God's character we think of
it in terms of Christ. When we think of God as creator we
think of him as the Father whose eternal Son was with him
from the foundation of the world. Similarly, 'when we speak of
the divine providence, we mean that the universe as a whole, as
well as in all its parts, is being sustained and ordered by the
wise, holy and loving end which Christ reveals' (W. Adams
Brown).

I can almost hear some of my readers saying, 'If ever there
was an affirmation of blind faith, that is it!' By the end of the
next chapter I shall have done my best to take due account of
the objections to the doctrine of providence. I shall also have
glanced at a few alternatives to it which I find much more
unacceptable than the doctrine itself. But in this chapter I wish
to affirm the doctrine; to say what it means; and to draw out
some of its religious implications.

Before going any further I think it is wise to make two points.
First, some theologians have spoken of general and special
providence. General providence is the general governance and
sustenance of the world by God; special providences are God's
(often dramatic) interventions in particular instances. If we
make too much of this distinction, however, we give a lever to
those who wish to say that whilst there is general providence in
the sense that by some means or another the laws of nature are
upheld, it is foolish to suppose that any deity is especially
concerned with particular events within the world. Foolish or
not, it is biblical. God cares for all—even for the sparrows
(Matt. 10: 29; Lk. 12: 6). It is best, then, to think of providence
as being all of a piece. Certainly this is most helpful from the
point of view of our religious life. If the Bible assures me that
Jesus loves *me*; that God forgives *my* sins, and so on, I cannot
rest satisfied with a theory which declares that such things
cannot be. As James Orr rightly said, 'It is a paltry conception,

this theory of a God who looks after the generalities of things, but does not attend to the details.'

William Jay was much nearer the mark. Reflecting upon the circumstances which led him to enter upon his pastorate of sixty-three years in Bath he said, 'The Lord determines the bounds of our habitations; and the events that move us from one place to another are as much under the direction of his providence, as the fiery cloudy pillar which was the conductor of the Israelites in the wilderness.' And in the course of the Confession of Faith which he delivered at his induction service Jay said that 'without an overruling providence we can have no confidence in the Supreme Being: if saints [i.e. Christians], we shall want [i.e. lack] the principal solace in adversity; if sinners, we shall want the principal restraint in prosperity. If we pervert this necessary doctrine by denying a particular providence, we destroy a particular confidence, a particular solace of comfort, a particular motive to duty, and give our actions only a general rule of reference.'

In similar vein Dr John Dick said that 'to a God who governed the world solely by general laws, we might have looked up with reverence, but not with the confidence, and gratitude, and hope, which arise from the belief that he superintends its minutest affairs. The thought that he "compasses our paths and is acquainted with all our ways;" that he watches our steps, and orders all the events in our lot; guides and protects us, and supplies our wants, as it were, with his own hand; this thought awakens a train of sentiments and feelings highly favourable to devotion, and sheds a cheering light upon the path of life. We consider him as our Guardian and our Father; and, reposing upon his care, we are assured that, if we trust in him, no evil shall befall us, and no real blessing shall be with-held.'

Secondly, there is the opposite, unhelpful, view that 'providences' are only special, dramatic interruptions of the normal course of events. Miracles have sometimes been regarded as special providences in this sense. Now we may certainly believe that God acts dramatically in history from time to time: the Cross-Resurrection event is the supreme example of this. If we call this a special divine intervention, we must not be misled by the word 'intervention' into thinking that God is an occasional visitor to his world only. Some events may be more dramatic than others, but God is working all the time. A clergyman, the sole survivor, once related his providential escape from a burning ship. Archbishop Whately commented, 'But last time I crossed the Channel, I had a far more providential experience. There were over five hundred of us, and would you believe it, the ship never once caught fire, and every one of us reached his destination in safety.' That is exactly the point.

It is easy to see why the 'miraculous' loomed so large in the minds of earlier theologians. They regarded miracles as *evidence* of God's existence. But Hume and others have taught us that whilst events which we cannot explain undoubtedly occur, it is a long hop from such events to a God as their cause. Most Christians nowadays would regard miracles as (in the word used for them in John's Gospel) *signs* to those who believe, rather than as evidence which may be presented to those who do not believe. The sceptic can always find an alternative explanation of the miraculous: the stilling of the storm was a pure coincidence (if, indeed, the event occurred at all); the feeding of the multitude was a 'miracle of sharing' in which each brought out his sandwiches—and so on. But to the believer such events are signs of, and witnesses to God's providential control and Fatherly care; but this control, this care, is affirmed because God the Father has approached us in Christ his Son. So much by way of ground-clearing.

I

The word 'providence' occurs once only in the Bible (Ac. 24: 2), and there it means 'foreknowledge'. Gradually the meaning of the term was extended to suggest that the God who foreknows is in control—otherwise what is foreknown would not come to pass. But although the word appears only once, the idea of providence is there throughout the scriptures. God is the 'Disposer Supreme, and Judge of the earth' (Jean-Baptiste de Santeüil). It is consistent with God's omnipresence that he should be in all as sustainer; it is consistent with his omniscience that he should know the needs of all, and with his omnipotence that he should be able to meet their needs and bring his purposes to pass. Indeed, 'providence' is shorthand for all of this: 'The providence of God keeps the whole creation upon the wheels' (Thomas Watson).

'Creatures, as numerous as they be,
   Are subject to Thy care;
There's not a place where we can flee,
   But God is present there.'

                 (Isaac Watts)

All of this is borne out by the Bible. Thus, God is said providentially to govern the physical order:

'Thou dost visit the earth and give it abundance,
   as often as thou dost enrich it
with the waters of heaven, brimming in their channels,
   providing rain for men.
For this is thy provision for it,
   watering its furrows, levelling its ridges,
softening it with showers and blessing its growth.'
(Ps. 65: 9-10; *cf.* Job 37: 6-13; Ps. 104: 14; 135: 6-7; 147:
                                15-17)

God watches over the animal creation:

'All of them look expectantly to thee
   to give them their food at the proper time;
what thou givest them they gather up;
   when thou openest thy hand, they eat their fill . . .'
               (Ps. 104: 27-28; *cf.* 147: 9)

God superintends trivial events:

'The lots may be cast into the lap,
   but the issue depends wholly on the Lord'
                  (Prov. 16: 33)

—and great ones:

'He changes seasons and times;
   he deposes kings and sets them up . . .'
                  (Dan. 2: 21)

As for men, God cares for all sorts and conditions; he 'makes his sun rise on good and bad alike, and sends the rain on the honest and the dishonest' (Matt. 5: 45). Psalm 107 contains a wonderful catalogue of God's providences. He rescued Israel out of troubles and distresses (vv. 4-6); he ministered to prisoners (vv. 10-12); he tended the sick (vv. 17-19); he is with storm-tossed sailors (v. 23), with the hungry (vv. 33-40), and with the poor (vv. 40-41).

But in a particular way God's providence is over his church. He sustains his people. As Paul said to the Philippians, 'it is God who works in you, inspiring both the will and the deed, for his own chosen purpose' (Phil. 2: 13). No wonder that the powers of death shall not conquer God's true church (Matt. 16: 18).

> 'Thy providence is kind and large,
>   Both man and beast Thy bounty share;
> The whole creation is Thy charge,
>   But saints are Thy peculiar care.'
>
>   (I. Watts)

Can it really be that God is interested in me, and not in creation at large, creatures in general, saints *en masse*? Does he care for me? Does he even know me? Can he hear my prayers? Has he a purpose for me? To all these questions the Bible answers with a resounding 'Yes!' As Jesus said, 'Are not sparrows two a penny? Yet without your Father's leave not one of them can fall to the ground. As for you, even the hairs of your head have all been counted. So have no fear; you are of more worth than any number of sparrows' (Matt. 10: 29-31). 'There is enough in the doctrine of God's providence to silence all the fears of God's people,' commented Matthew Henry: 'If God numbers their hairs, much more does he number their heads, and take care of their lives, their comforts, their souls.' In Augustine's memorable phrase, 'He loves us every one as though there were but one of us to love,' The exhortation is, then, 'Cast all your cares on him, for you are his charge' (I Pet. 5: 7).

> 'The Lord shall keep thy soul; He shall
>   Preserve thee from all ill;

Henceforth thy going out and in
  God keep for ever will.'

(F. Rous and W. Barton)

Now this optimism is no free and easy thing. We cannot say,
'God is in charge; all is well; therefore I need do nothing.' The
Bible always associates assurance with obedience; with being
ready to face all for, and with, God (Matt. 10: 28, 33; Lk. 12:
4,10). As a matter of fact it was as Paul contemplated all that
had flowed from the *Cross* (no bed of roses that!) that he was
able to see providence everywhere else, and to know that 'all
things work together for good to them that love God' (Rom. 8:
28, A.V.). Paul 'sees, as it were, the vast, over-arching firmament
of providence reflected in the narrow waters of his own soul. He
knows that the wisdom and love which are meeting him so
livingly and savingly within the chaos and complexity of his own
life, rule over all, and may be trusted to work just as victoriously
within the chaos and complexity of universal history' (H. H.
Farmer). In a nutshell, then, the Christian doctrine of
providence is that

'There is an overruling Providence
  That wisely marshals every circumstance;
Heaven, air, and seas, and this terrestrial ball,
  With their contents, are all at His control.

There's not a particle of dust can fly,
  A sparrow fall, or cloud obscure the sky,
A moth be crushed, or leaf fall from a tree,
  But in submission to His wise decree.

He raiseth men to sceptres and a crown,
  And at His pleasure treads the monarch down;
His wise decrees as firm as heaven do stand;
  He's in one mind, tho' oft He turns His hand.

He must and will at all times keep in view,
  His glory and His people's welfare, too;
Bright days, dark nights, the furnace or the flood,
  He overrules for Zion's real good.'

(H. H. Lawson)

II

Having said what the Christian doctrine of providence is, I shall now draw out some of its religious implications.

The doctrine of the providence of the God we know in Christ keeps us humble. This humility does not always come easily to us. The sin of Adam and Eve (Gen. 3) was the proud one of thinking that they knew better than God; that their purposes were more satisfactory than his. Naaman, the successful and well-known Syrian general who was smitten with leprosy, is a further classic instance of a man who thought he knew best. The prophet Elisha, no respecter of persons, did not meet Naaman personally. He sent a messenger to him with the instruction, 'If you will go and wash seven times in the Jordan, your flesh will be restored and you will be clean' (II Kgs. 5: 10). Naaman was furious: 'I thought he would at least have come out and stood, and invoked the Lord his God by name, waved his hand over the place and so rid me of the disease. Are not Abana and Pharpar, rivers of Damascus, better than all the waters of Israel? Can I not wash in them and be clean?' (II Kgs. 5: 11-12).

Again, the rich young ruler who came to Jesus was sure that there must have been a way of following Christ which did not involve the sacrifice of his material possessions—would not his law-keeping suffice? (Matt. 19: 16-22; Lk. 18: 18-23). To the Jews it seemed incredible that the *Messiah* should die a criminal's death—they would not have arranged things that way. The Zealots among them would have had a quite different sort of Messiah anyway: not one who 'stormed' Jerusalem riding an animal of peace. Even Jesus, in agony in the garden of Gethsemane prayed, 'My Father'—he still called God 'Father'—'if it be possible, let this cup pass me by.' But he at once added, 'Yet not as I will, but as thou wilt' (Matt. 26: 39; Mk. 14: 36; Lk. 22: 42). Here we see supremely that humble acquiescence in the will of God which prompts resignation; and from resignation flows contentment.

No doubt Paul would have preferred not to have been imprisoned, stoned, shipwrecked, flogged; but by grace he trusted in the divine providence, so that he could say, 'I have learned, in whatsoever state I am, therein to be content' (Phil. 4: 11). Anne Brontë, who died at the age of twenty-nine, learned the same lesson: 'I hoped,' she wrote,

> 'That with the brave and strong
>   My portioned task might lie;
> To toil amid the busy throng
>   With purpose pure and high;
> But God has fixed another part,
>   And He has fixed it well,
> I said so with my breaking heart,
>   When first this trouble fell.'

These lines emphasise the hardness of the lesson. We are baffled—even outraged. We cannot understand, but by faith we believe that there *is* a purpose; and with John Flavel we agree that 'Some providences, like Hebrew letters, must be read backwards.' Or, in Watson's image, 'The wheels in a clock seem to move contrary one to the other, but they help forward the motion of the clock, and make the larum strike: so the providences of God seem to be cross wheels; but for all that, they shall carry on the good of the elect.'

Sometimes our lack of humble resignation is so colossal that we become blatant hypocrites. We boldly sing Newman's lines,

> 'I do not ask to see
> The distant scene; one step enough for me'—

when all the time we are developing ulcers precisely because we can *not* see the distant scene. How we need the humble resignation of Job: 'He knoweth the way that I take' (Job 23: 10, A.V.)! Indeed, with how much more conviction than Job ought Christians to be able to say that! For the risen Christ goes on before us, the 'pioneer and perfecter of our faith' (Heb. 12: 2, R.S.V.). And the Christian, in his better moments, knows that

> 'Christ leads me through no darker rooms
>   Than He went through before;
> He that into God's kingdom comes
>   Must enter by this door.'
>
>   (Richard Baxter)

In his more despondent moments the Christian recalls that

> '... nothing falls unknown to Him,
>   Of care or joy or sorrow,
> And He, whose mercy ruled the past,
>   Will be our stay tomorrow.'
>   (A. N. Blatchford)

We must always beware, however, of confusing humble resignation with fatalistic acquiescence. 'Whatever will be, will be' can be said in thoroughly non-Christian tones. Christians should be ever ready to counter the caricature of the doctrine of providence which Julian Huxley expressed thus: 'Divine Providence is an excuse for the poor whom we will always have with us; for the inhuman improvidence which produces whole broods of children without reflection or care as to how they shall live; for not taking action when we are lazy; or, more rarely, for justifying the action we do take when we are energetic.' In fact Christians have been to the fore in the alleviation of pain; in the securing of a fair deal for the hungry, the homeless, the illiterate, the imprisoned, the worker; and some of the most searching of prophetic denunciations of God's people in every age have been prompted by their failures in these matters. We cannot follow Christ and be unconcerned for the needy and the oppressed (Matt. 25: 31-46). Righteous indignation against wrong is not abnormal in a Christian; it is profoundly normal.

Again, as I said in a previous chapter, the fact that God's providence is over all should not inhibit our peititionary prayer. We should not say, 'Because God already knows, I need not ask.' We have the privilege of a Father-Son relationship: let us enjoy it. And if we ask and do not receive, the doctrine of providence will save us from petulance or despair: 'Though Providence does not yet perform the mercies you wait for, yet you have no ground to entertain hard thoughts of God, for it is possible God never gave you any ground for your expectation of these things from Him' (John Flavel). God's providence works in accordance with his purpose for all men. Our perception of what that purpose is can never be complete, and at times it may be deficient in the extreme. We need to be able to say with Whittier,

> 'All as God wills, who wisely heeds
>   To give or to withhold,
> And knoweth more of all my needs
>   Than all my prayers have told.'

A true grasp of the divine providence enables us confidently to trust in God at all times and in all circumstances. The story is often told of Bulstrode Whitelocke, a diplomat in Cromwellian times. In 1653 he was in Sweden on a mission, and all was far from well at home. He was restless and could get no sleep. Eventually his servant asked him a question: 'Sir, did God govern the world well before you came into it?' 'Undoubtedly,' replied Whitelocke. 'And will He rule the world when you have gone out of it?' 'Undoubtedly.' 'Then, sir, can you not trust Him to rule the world well while you are in it?' And Bulstrode Whitelocke went to sleep. He began to trust once more, and from trust came peace.

God's ancient people had fallen upon hard times. Large numbers of them had been carried off into captivity in Babylon. To them home was a mere memory; they longed to return. The faithful among them longed to worship in the house of the Lord once more, but there seemed little hope of that. In their dejection they sang laments:

> 'By the rivers of Babylon we sat down and wept
>   when we remembered Zion.
> There on the willow-trees
>   we hung our harps,
> for there those who carried us off
>   demanded music and singing,
> and our captors called on us to be merry:
>   "Sing us one of the songs of Zion."
> How could we sing the Lord's song
>   in a foreign land?'

(Ps. 137: 1-4)

But if they could not sing of the Lord, the Lord was watching over them. That was Deutero-Isaiah's message to them. They shall go home. As God had rescued their fathers from Egypt so, in time, he would rescue them. God's 'saving power will never wane'. Meanwhile they should take heart. Oppression will not have the last word with them, nor will it last much longer. God still says to them, 'You are my people' (Isa. 51: 16). This is all of a piece with Jesus's challenge. He did not forbid us to make plans, but he did forbid anxious thought. Why? Because God knows; God cares; his providence is over all (Matt. 6: 25-34).

> 'What Thou shalt to-day provide
>   Let me as a child receive;
> What tomorrow may betide
>   Calmly to Thy wisdom leave:
> 'Tis enough that Thou wilt care;
>   Why should I the burden bear?'
>
> (John Newton)

From trust comes patience. It is important for us to remember that 'The Lord does not compute and reckon His seasons by the working of our arithmetic' (John Flavel). However long the delay we know that God's victory is assured, and that

> 'Not one promise shall miscarry;
>   Not one blessing come too late;'

and we go on to ask,

> 'Though the vision long may tarry,
>   Give us patience, Lord, to wait.'
>
> (Jane Crewdson)

In any case, to return to our starting point, we cannot overrule the Almighty. As John Bunyan lay in prison he wrote, 'Here I lie waiting the good will of God to do with me as He pleaseth, knowing that not one hair of my head can fall to the ground without the will of my Father who is in heaven; that, let the rage and malice of men be what they may, they can do no more and go no farther than God permits them; and even when they have done their worst, we know that all things work together for good for them that love God.'

> 'Sovereign Ruler of the skies,
>   Ever gracious, ever wise;
> All my times are in Thy hand,
> All events at Thy command.'

> (John Ryland)

Is not this cause for gratitude? John Flavel thought so, and in his book *The Mystery of Providence* (1678) he lists five grounds of praise connected with providence. We have reason to praise God when we note his mercies; when we remember them; when they do us good; when we acknowledge them; and when we offer all he gives back to him. But there is a sixth ground of praise which I would express, after the manner of Flavel, thus: 'A due appreciation and valuation of every providence that *appears* to do us harm.' There is no doubt that such providences come. Of Christ Thomas Watson said, 'Was his head crowned with thorns, and do we think to be crowned with roses? . . . Every print of the rod is a badge of honour . . . The magnet of mercy does not draw us so near to God as the cords of affliction.' But is it really so? Is not the suggestion too good to be true that we can praise God despite suffering? Is not suffering itself an insuperable obstacle to belief in the divine providence? Many would agree that it is, and the question cannot for ever be held at bay. We shall investigate it in the next chapter. But there is no need, meanwhile, for the Christian to be deflected from praise and prayer.

* * * * *

A Hymn:

> 'A fulness resides in Jesus our Head,
>   And ever abides to answer our need;
> The Father's good pleasure has laid up in store
>   A plentiful treasure to give to the poor.

> Whate'er be our wants, we need not to fear;
>   Our numerous complaints His mercy will hear;
> His fulness shall yield us abundant supplies;
>   His power shall shield us when dangers arise.

The fountain o'erflows our woes to redress,
   Still more He bestows, and grace upon grace:
His gifts in abundance we daily receive;
   He has a redundance for all that believe.

Whatever distress awaits us below,
   Such plentiful grace will Jesus bestow,
As still shall support us, and silence our fear;
   For nothing can hurt us while Jesus is near.

When troubles attend, or danger, or strife,
   His love will defend and guard us through life:
And when we are fainting, and ready to die,
   Whatever is wanting, His grace will supply.'

(John Fawcett)

A Prayer:

'Hold us fast, O Lord of Hosts, that we fall not from Thee; grant us thankful and obedient hearts, that we may increase daily in the love, knowledge, and fear of Thee; increase our faith, and help our unbelief, that we, being provided for and relieved in all our needs by Thy Fatherly care and providence, as Thou shalt think good, may live a godly life, to the praise and good example of Thy people, and after this life may reign with Thee for ever, through Christ our Saviour. Amen.'

(Bishop James Pilkington, A.D. 1520)

7

The Balm of Life, The Cure of Woe

Paul said that God works all things together for good to those who love him (Rom. 8: 28). Despite the doubts and fears which sometimes assail them, it is those who love him who know that this is true. To the unbeliever it is all so irritatingly circular: if you love God you believe in his providence, if you do not love him, you do not. This is by no means to say that the Christian can give no reasons for his trust in God's providence; but his reasons will always take the form of a more or less orderly account of the faith by which he lives.

But the unbeliever is in precisely the same state. He too has a kind of faith. He too has his presuppositions, his starting-point. His *conviction* is that there is no God, and hence no divine providence. To the Epicurean, for example, the world was governed by chance, caprice. The gods (if any) were quite unconcerned about men, and to worship them was to grovel. Calvin contrasted this attitude—by no means confined to ancient Greece—with that of the Christian believer: 'If one falls among robbers, or ravenous beasts; if a sudden gust of wind at sea causes shipwreck; if one is struck down by the fall of a house or a tree; if another, when wandering through desert paths, meets with deliverance; or, after being tossed by the waves, arrives in port, and makes some wondrous hairbreadth escape from death—all these occurrences, prosperous as well as adverse, carnal sense will attribute to fortune. But whoso has learned from the mouth of Christ that all the hairs of his head are numbered (Matt. 10: 30), will look farther for the cause, and hold that all events whatsoever are governed by the secret counsel of God.'

Zeno and the Stoics, on the other hand, had a different starting-point. They held that the world was governed by necessity, Fate; all was determined. There is an inexorability here in face of which man is powerless. He may as well submit to the mindless arrangment, for 'the Fates lead the willing, the unwilling they drag' (Seneca). *The* virtue is submission. Again, in our own time some have held that the universe just is; it is a brute fact. The question of its governance is not a proper question: it makes no sense to raise it. If life is to be tolerable the onus is upon man to make it so. The presence of so many rival political and other theories amply testifies to the fact that this is easier said than done.

Since the three statements, 'All is in the hands of Chance,' 'All is at the disposal of Fate,' and 'The question of the governance of the world is a non-question' are all affirmations of faith from which men start out on their intellectual pilgrimages, the Christian may, with a due measure of godly defiance, pit his affirmation against the rest. Joseph Irons, for example, spoke of the "wheel of providence", and threw down the gauntlet thus:

'Let atheists vainly talk of chance,
    I would this wheel adore,
Which rules and guides each circumstance
    Which angels can't explore.'

I am suggesting, then, that the fact of the divine providence cannot rationally be demonstrated to an unbeliever. Equally, *he* cannot produce a logically coercive proof of the validity of his stance. One sets out from an axiom, and then the attempt may be made to show that what follows from it is coherent, takes due account of the facts of the case, is less exposed to difficulties than alternative positions, and so on. The Christian believes that the doctrine of the providence of the Fatherly God of holy love whom we know in Christ is preferable to alternative theories. Indeed, it is the only view which makes the agonies of life tolerable, and offers ground for hope.

But is not the claim just made wishful thinking? The Christian himself may sometimes be tempted to think that it is. There are both intellectual and moral obstacles to the doctrine of the divine providence. The former concern human actions in relation to God's providence; the latter gather under the name of the problem of evil. Let us look at each group of problems in turn.

I

If God is in control, can man act freely? When man acts sinfully, is not God responsible if he is in control—and how can *God*, the holy One, be responsible for sin? These are the questions posed to the intellect by the doctrine of divine providence.

The first point to be made is that the word 'freedom' is used in more than one way in theology. Sometimes it is used of man's unbound will. This is the freedom of which Charles Wesley sang:

> 'My chains fell off, my heart was free—
> I rose, went forth, and followed thee.'

He had been a prisoner, a captive to sin; but now, by the grace of God he was free. This was the freedom which Luther extolled. He maintained that a man is free to act in accordance with his nature. But if his will is bound, he cannot perform actions, or make choices, which are truly pleasing to God. For that his will needs to be freed.

However, Wesley and Luther—and, for that matter, Augustine—recognised that man is free in another sense of the word. He has the power of 'contrary choice' over a wide range of daily decisions. He is not absolutely free, of course. He cannot decide to fly, or to live for a long time unaided on the sea bed. But in many circumstances of life he can decide to do this rather than that. He is therefore a responsible being; he is accountable; he will be judged.

At the same time, God's providence is over all. So what of the situation in which a man makes a sinful choice and acts wrongly? Is God really the author of sin? Jesus, who had done no wrong, was crucified, and the book of Acts makes no bones about it: 'Herod and Pontius Pilate conspired with the Gentiles and peoples of Israel to do all things which, under thy hand and by thy decree, were foreordained' (4: 27-28). It seems undeniable that God permitted evil to occur, and equally undeniable that he overruled the evil for good. Now as Matthew Henry realised, 'Sin is not the less evil for God's bringing good out of it, but by this he is the more glorified.'

But even if it be true that good *always* results from evil, the philosophical difficulty is not thereby resolved. For would it not be better if there were no evil in the first place? I cannot see that there is a watertight solution available to our finite minds. Nor, for example, could William Jay. His physician wrote after his pastor's death: 'one day speaking of Judas, he said he was foreordained of God to betray the Saviour, and yet he betrayed Him willingly, and is damned for the deed:—having said so, he, in his own peculiar and well-known manner, leaned over the pulpit, and exclaimed, "Now, do not look at me for an explanation of this subject—both statements are true—the foreknowledge of God, and the free agency of man; and when we reach heaven, and not till then, shall we be able to understand all, which in our present imperfect condition is quite beyond the grasp of our finite minds."'

If a completely satisfactory explanation eludes us, perhaps Dr Miall Edwards's illustration may help a little: 'A passenger on board a ship has innumerable possibilities of voluntary actions open to him—he can walk about on deck, play certain games, converse, read, think his own thoughts, watch the waves, etc. etc.—and it makes a real difference to his comfort and self-respect that within limits he is at liberty to "do what he likes." Yet his free movements cannot frustrate the whole plan of the ship's course as controlled by the captain. A mad, rebellious passenger might suppose that he was thwarting that plan, so far as he himself was involved in it, by walking on deck in the direction opposite to that taken by the ship; but there are obvious limits to his powers in that way. More accurately, we are not mere passengers on board the ship of the universe, but members of the crew . . . A mutiny of the crew may have serious consequences; but we may well believe that, with the infinitely greater resources which the Captain has at His disposal, His larger ends will ultimately be realized. It is tempting to pursue the illustration further, but this may suffice to elucidate the view that there may be room in the universe at once for a real though limited human freedom and for an overruling divine Providence.'

If we fail to hold together God's providence and man's freedom we detract from both God and man. God loses his sovereignty, and man his responsibility, his humanness. Man could then excuse his sin by saying that God must have intended him to be a sinner; and one of whom that were true would have no use for a Saviour. Robert Shaw put the point in a nutshell: 'We are certain that God is concerned in all the actions of his creatures; we are equally certain that God cannot be the author of sin; and here we ought to rest.'

But if the intellectual puzzles concerning man's free—and especially his sinful—actions in relation to God's providence tease us, the problem of evil agonises us. To this problem, or cluster of problems, I now turn, with Milton's words ringing in my ears:

> '   What in me is dark
> Illumine, what is low raise and support;
> That to the height of this great argument
> I may assert eternal Providence
> And justify the ways of God to Men.'

II

'We lived several years in a state of much happiness,' declared Oliver Goldsmith's Vicar of Wakefield, 'not but that we sometimes had those little rubs which Providence sends to enhance the value of its favours. My orchard was often robbed by school-boys, and my wife's custards plundered by the cats or the children. The 'Squire would sometimes fall asleep in the most pathetic parts of my sermon ... But we soon got over the uneasiness caused by such accidents, and usually in three or four days began to wonder how they vext us.' I should think so! The only puzzle is why it took them so long to recover from such 'evils'. In comparison with the Vicar's pin-pricks, some evils fall like sledge-hammer blows. 'Where was God when six million Jews were being slaughtered?' 'Why did God allow my daughter to be killed in a road accident?' Questions of this kind cross the minds of all rational people who are not made of stone.

Job, the upright man, suffered grievously. He lost his family and his possessions, and the questions came flooding in. He was quite unable to accept the verdict of his 'comforters' that his suffering was the punishment for sins committed. He was a God-honouring man. The received theological explanation just did not fit. Job's battle was long and hard. Often he was near to despair:

> 'My thoughts today are resentful,
> for God's hand is heavy on me in my trouble.
> If only I knew how to find him,
> how to enter his court,
> I would state my case before him
> and set out my arguments in full;
> then I should learn what answer he would give
> and find out what he had to say.'

(Job 23: 2-5)

Even a Psalmist can verge upon cynicism: 'Dost thou work wonders for the dead?' (Ps. 88: 10).

Macbeth sought reassurance that life is more than

> '...A tale
> Told by an idiot, full of sound and fury,
> Signifying nothing.'

If Job and the Psalmist could have believed that that was all life was, their agony would have been less acute. But they were *believers*. It was precisely because of their commitment to the God of love and power that their distress was so great. Their question was not 'Why is life like this?' but 'How can *God* allow this?' They faced the dilemma which Augustine was later to pose thus: 'Either God cannot abolish evil or he will not: if he cannot then he is not all-powerful; if he will not then he is not all-good.' What we need, and what I believe we have, is a theodicy—a justification of the ways of God to men.

As I said, 'the problem of evil' is an umbrella term. It shelters a number of problems. In the first place, 'evil' is not all of one kind. We may think of two main classes of evils, natural and moral. In the first class come pain and suffering. We can see some point in some pain. If the toddler did not feel pain when putting his fingers into the flame he might burn himself to death. But often the amount of pain seems out of all proportion. It is no longer merely a warning; and sometimes it comes too late for remedial action to be taken. It is clear that whilst for much pain man can be blamed, for much he can not. Can God be blamed?

Suffering is painful too, but we often think of suffering as being something wider than personal, individual pain. We think of millions of refugees; of men and women imprisoned for their faith; of those who live in war-torn lands. We think too of the apparently random and pointless suffering which results from earthquake, tornado, flood. It is not difficult to understand J. S. Mill's outburst: 'Nearly all the things which men are hanged or imprisoned for doing to one another, are nature's every day performances.' Nature acts 'with the most supercilious disregard both of mercy and of justice.' 'What a book a devil's chaplain might write on the clumsy, wasteful, blundering, low, and horribly cruel works of nature,' said Darwin. As for Stendhal, his verdict was that 'God's only excuse is that he does not exist'.

To those who suffer as a result of man's inhumanity to man, or because of nature's red-in-tooth-and-claw-ness it comes as cold comfort to be told that after all some men are pleasant, and not all of nature is nasty. It is little more than an evasion to extol the glories of a sunset in such circumstances, or to point out that in 1809, when men were being slaughtered in the Napoleonic Wars, 'God sent babies'—Gladstone, Tennyson, Mendelssohn and Lincoln, to name but a few. Nor does it solve the problem of the existence of suffering in the first place to point out that often people have risen to the height of courage, and have made their most telling witness in face of great suffering. The statement is true enough, but it is also true that on many other occasions suffering has embittered an individual's life and stunted his spiritual growth. The Stoics would have agreed with the Cambridge Platonist Ralph

Cudworth that 'a doubtful and cloudy state of things' enables 'the better exercise of virtue and faith.' The trouble is that it does not always do this; or, at least, it does not do it for everybody.

Sceptics will rightly be even less satisfied with Christian attempts to turn the question round upon them. 'You say you have difficulty in relating God and evil? But how would you account for *good* apart from God?' Sadly for those who pose this question, the person puzzled by evil is puzzled precisely because it is alleged that as well as evil there is a good, loving God. From his own point of view he is under no obligation to account for good: he can just accept it as it comes and enjoy it. Neither by attempting to turn the question round, nor by describing noble ways in which evil has been responded to, can the Christian side-step the question, 'Why the evil in the first place?'

Evil offends the moral sense. Men are outraged by its apparent randomness, and by the inequitability of its distribution. So often it comes without warning and without desert. Why do wars start here and not there? Why is one land smitten by natural disaster, and another not? As Voltaire asked, why did Paris escape whereas Lisbon was devastated by the earthquake of 1755? It is not even the bad alone that suffer. On the contrary, often 'the wicked grow like grass and every evil doer prospers'—at least *pro tem* (Ps. 92: 7).

But this reference to 'the bad' brings us to the other aspect of evil: moral evil. However the entry of sin into the world is to be explained—and we can only assume that God's purposes will best be accomplished in a world in which men are free to love him or to spurn his love and disobey his commands—the fact is that there is an out-of-sorts-ness in men and things which is a witness to alienation from God.

It would, of course, be foolish to say that we can never answer the question 'Why did this happen to me?' If a man spends many years abusing his body with great dedication, so that in the end he is riddled with disease, we are not, when confronted by the question 'Why?' faced by one of life's great mysteries. We have a cause-effect situation. We know (and usually the sufferer knows) why he is as he is. We do not say that God has sent the disease to punish him; we say that the disease is the inevitable consequence of his living as he has done.

More frequently, perhaps, the answer to the question 'Why?' is, 'I do not know.' Certainly it is often necessary to allay any fear on the part of a sufferer that his suffering *is* a direct consequence of his sins. But the question presses: even if man is a sinner, why the colossal amount of evil? Why the imbalance throughout the world? It is the same question which arose in connection with natural evil. Natural and moral evil seem to be on a par at this point. Together they seem to bear witness to a radical disharmony in which both nature and man are involved. Paul writes that 'up to the present, we know, the whole created universe groans in all its parts as if in the pangs of childbirth. Not only so, but even we, to whom the Spirit is given as firstfruits of the harvest to come, are groaning inwardly while we wait for God to make us his sons and set our whole body free' (Rom. 8: 22-23). The idea is that 'nature is in a state of arrested development through sin, is frustrated of its true end, and has a destiny before it which sin does not permit it to attain. There is an arrest... which begets in the creature a sense of bondage, and an earnest longing for deliverance' (James Orr).

Thomas Hardy's Tess answered her little brother's question about the happiness or blightedness of our world by saying, 'Ours is a blighted one.' It is certainly blemished; but is all finally doomed? Are we shut up to unrelieved pessimism? Does God care?

III

Christianity affirms that he does. In making this affirmation Christianity sets its face against a number of alternative 'solutions' to the problem of evil which have been offered. First, as I said in the chapter on creation, Christianity will have no truck with dualism. As far as the problem of evil is concerned this means that Christians cannot think in terms of two equal gods, one benevolent and one demonic, nor even of a supreme deity eternally opposed to a lesser, malevolent deity. Nor again may evil be attributed to matter (conceived as evil), or to any deficiency within God. It was precisely because of a desire to shun dualism that many thinkers (with more than a nod in the direction of Plato and Plotinus), including Augustine—the erstwhile Manichaean dualist—Erigena, Aquinas and Leibniz, refused to allow that evil had any independent existence at all. They called it a privation of good. That is to say, for example, that the inability to walk would, in a man, be an evil; for a man is supposed to be able to walk. The inability to walk would not be an evil in the case of a stone. Evil, then, is the absence of a good which ought to be present. It is parasitic upon good. It is real enough in the world of every-day, but it has no ultimate status or durability. The hostility between good and evil which we undoubtedly see in the world around, and know in ourselves, is ultimately to be ended in favour of good. Indeed, says the Christian, in the Cross-Resurrection event the battle has in principle already been won. It remains only to add that dualism fails in any case to answer the question 'Why evil?' It simply pushes the questioning farther back. We now need to know 'Why the malevolent deity?' 'Why (evil) matter?'

Secondly, Christianity has traditionally turned its back upon pluralism, and for good reason. Pluralists teach that God, the first among equals, is limited by other and alien beings. Against these God struggles to achieve his purposes, and he invites us to join him in the battle. This view seems to undermine all that Christianity wishes to say about God's sovereignty, and on this view we would have no grounds for expecting or even hoping that good would ultimately triumph. The Christian can only bluntly say, 'This is not how God has made himself known in the scriptures, in Christ, or to me.'

Thirdly, Christianity cannot agree with those who claim that evil is really illusory. On the contrary, it unreservedly accepts the grim reality of evil as being something vanquished and to be vanquished. Unlike some oriental philosophies; unlike Spinoza, who thought that if we got our thinking straight we would see that evil is illusory; unlike Christian Science, Christianity affirms the reality of pain, suffering, and sin. Indeed, they are only too real. They involve a Cross. And there at the Cross God's love and God's power are shown, and are active.

With the mention of the Cross we come to the threshold of the Christian answer to the problem of evil—or rather, perhaps, the Christian testimony in face of evil. This is not surprising. My whole object in this book is to show that if we wish to see the Christian God, we must begin from Christ, his greatest revelation to man; if we wish to know what God is like—that he is Father, that he loves us, and so on—we must see him in Christ his Son; if we wish to understand, however partially, God's character and his works, we must view all in the light of his revelation in Christ. If God is going to give us anything to say in face of evil, he will give it in Christ; and he does.

But it is very important that we understand what kind of an answer we have in Christ. It is not the kind of answer which will remove all the intellectual problems of which I have spoken; nor will it remove our sense of outrage against evil and inequity. As far as all that is concerned Lotze was right: 'No one,' he said, 'has here found the thought which would save us from our difficulty, and I too know it not.'

The Christian answer is an intensely practical answer. It builds upon the Old Testament experience of Job. One of the most significant things about Job is that after his ordeal he was, in an intellectual sense, none the wiser. He still did not know *why* he had suffered; but he knew God:

> 'I know that thou canst do all things
> and that no purpose is beyond thee.
> But I have spoken of great things which I
>   have not understood,
> things too wonderful for me to know.
> I knew of thee then only by report,
> but now I see thee with my own eyes.
> Therefore I melt away;
> I repent in dust and ashes.'

(Job 42: 2-6)

For the man of faith fellowship with God was enough.

The Old Testament goes no further than this. But the New Testament does. It tells of the Fatherly God of holy love who comes in his Son Jesus Christ to seek and to save the lost. The Christ bears the worst that the sin of man could do, and vanquishes all by holy love. This is the meaning of the Cross-Resurrection event. So it is that Christians believe that if there never was a blacker day than the first Good Friday; and if God overcame *then*, how much more will he not overcome all the evils which smite us? If we by God's grace are his adopted sons, he will keep us; there is literally nothing in the world which can separate us from so strong a love (Rom. 8: 38-39). The Cross-Resurrection event is the once-for-all paradigm case of God's eternal victory. From this the Christian draws his hope of that life where 'there shall be an end to death, and to mourning and crying and pain' (Rev. 21: 4). Small wonder that Thomas Kelly called the Cross

> 'The balm of life, the cure of woe,
> The measure and the pledge of love,
> The sinner's refuge here below,
> The angels' theme in heaven above'.

Many great theological books have been written during this century. But one of the bravest, surely, was P. T. Forsyth's *The Justification of God*. It was written during the dark days of the First World War. Thousands were being slain; evil and horror were rampant; and many were asking, 'How can there be a good, loving God if all this can happen?' Forsyth courageously replied in words to this effect, 'If there is a God of *holy* love, and if men wilfully and persistently thwart him, what else would you expect but all this?' But that is not all he said. I shall conclude this section with a brief anthology of some of his remarks—no one has made the points better—and in the final section I shall draw out some practical implications.

> 'The final theodicy is in no discovered system, no revealed plan, but in an effected redemption. It is not in the grasp of ideas, nor in the adjustment of events, but in the destruction of guilt and the taking away of the sin of the world ... Our faith did not arise from the order of the world; the world's convulsion, therefore, need not destroy it ... We believe that all is well, even if all goes not well ... All is well with the world, since its Saviour has it finally and fully in hand. Victory awaits us because victory is won ... The thing is done, it is not to do. "Be of good cheer, I *have* overcome the world." ... The solution is

practical, not philosophical. It is not really an answer to a riddle, but a victory in a battle... Christianity is not the sacrifice we make, but the sacrifice we trust; not the victory we win, but the victory we inherit... We do not see the answer; we trust the Answerer, and measure by Him. We do not gain the victory; we are united with the Victor... The evil world will not win at last, because it failed to win at the only time it ever could. It is a vanquished world where men play their devilries. Christ has overcome it. It can make tribulation, but desolation it can never make.'

IV

So to three practical implications:

1. Because of Christ's vanquishing of evil the Christian may believe in the ultimate victory of good over evil. This is no bland optimism—bland is what one can never be at the foot of the Cross. Nor is it calling evil good. Rather, it is a testimony to God's overruling providence. He can and he does bring victory out of defeat, and turn the wrath of man to his praise (Ps. 76: 10). As Dr Orr said of the sinner, 'Refusing to serve God in one way, he will find himself forced to serve him in another.'

There are many examples of this in the Bible. Joseph was sold into slavery in Egypt by his brothers, but rose to become Chancellor at a time of famine, and even become the means of saving the lives of his brothers who came to Egypt to buy grain. This was Joseph's verdict on his brothers' act: 'You meant to do me harm; but God meant to bring good out of it by preserving the lives of many people, as we see today' (Gen. 50: 20). Peter and John boldly declared that God 'has given the highest honour to his servant Jesus, whom you [the Jews] committed for trial and repudiated in Pilate's court' (Ac. 3: 13). It was the persecution of the Jerusalem church which caused its members to scatter and gossip the gospel (Ac. 8: 4) to considerable effect (Ac. 11: 19-21). And very often in post-biblical times the blood of the martyrs has been the seed of the Church—or, as Gregory of Nazianzum said, the Church is that plant which lives by dying and grows by cutting.

But I do not speak of past events only. I firmly believe that
God can work through all the evils which befall *me*. The
doctrine of providence must apply to each one, or it applies to
no one. Few are as strong on this theme as the Puritans. Here is
John Flavel once more:

> 'when the world smiles upon us, and we have got a warm
> nest, how do we prophesy of rest and peace in those
> acquisitions, thinking, with good Baruch, great things for
> ourselves; but Providence by a particular or general
> calamity overturns our plans (Jer. 45: 4-5), and all this to
> turn our hearts from the creature to God, who is our only
> rest.'

Again, Bunyan spoke out of much experience when he reminded
the readers of his *Seasonable Counsel; or, Advice to Sufferers*
that 'we should be overgrown with flesh if we had not our
seasonable winters'. For his part William Bridge brought a
scientific principle to bear: 'Take the water as it is in the sea,
and it is salt and brackish; but drawn up by the sun into the
clouds, it becomes sweet, and falls down as sweet rain. So take
an affliction in itself, and it is salt and brackish; but drawn up
by divine love, then it is sweet.' As we might expect, Thomas
Watson was his usual characteristically pithy self: 'What if we
have more of the rough file, if we have less rust! . . . The magnet
of mercy does not draw us so near to God as the cords of
affliction . . . When God lays men upon their backs, then they
look up to heaven.'

The amazing thing is that even our own follies can be
redeemed! In Shakespeare's words,

> 'Our indiscretion sometimes serves us well,
> When our deep plots do pall; and that should teach us
> There's a divinity that shapes our ends,
> Rough-hew them how we will.'

Or, as we find it more succinctly in the book of *Proverbs*,

> 'A man's heart may be full of schemes,
> but the Lord's purpose will prevail.'
>
> (19: 21)

2. Because of Christ's victory the Christian may glorify God
in his sufferings, knowing that they will not have the last word

with him. Like Habakkuk of old, though with more reason, the Christian may sing,

> 'Though vine nor fig-tree neither
> Their wonted fruit should bear,
> Though all the field should wither,
> Nor flocks nor herds be there,
> Yet, God the same abiding,
> His praise shall tune my voice;
> For, while in Him confiding,
> I cannot but rejoice.'
>
> (William Cowper; cf. Hab. 3: 17-19)

After all, 'Christ suffered on your behalf, and thereby left you an example; it is for you to follow in his steps' (I Pet. 2: 21). How Paul rejoiced in the sufferings he bore for Christ (II Cor. 12: 10), knowing as he did that 'we are God's heirs and Christ's fellow-heirs, if we share his sufferings now in order to share his splendour hereafter' (Rom. 8: 17).

Even death itself is an occasion of testimony to the true Christian. Granted that some of the death-bed reports from bygone days make rather stilted reading, there was a point in our fathers' desire to 'make a happy death,' and in John Wesley's comment on his followers, 'Our people die well.' 'How it strikes a damp into wicked men, when they see that the godly will keep close to God in a suffering condition, and that, when they lose all, they yet will hold fast their integrity' (Thomas Watson). As the celebrated French preacher Adolphe Monod lay dying he said to those about his bedside, 'What consolation for those who suffer, to be able to say... I can, by these very sufferings render to God a glory which I would not be able to render otherwise.'

The Christian then need not fear. It cannot be a sad thing to go home to Christ whose love never lets us go.

> 'Art thou afraid His power shall fail
> When comes thy evil day?
> And can an all-creating arm
> Grow weary or decay?'

—asks Isaac Watts. And back comes Richard Burnham's reply:

'Shines the whole Providence of God,
    With love Divinely bright;
Whether He gives, with-holds, or takes,
    All is supremely right.'

Then let the Christian rejoice!

3. Because of Christ's victory the Christian may, even in
suffering, experience a 'peace which passes understanding' (Phil.
4: 7), and exult in the hope of an inheritance which 'nothing can
destroy or spoil or wither' (I Pet. 1: 4). It is, of course,
somewhat reassuring to reflect that the greatest and most valiant
have been assailed by Bunyan's Giant Despair. Martin Luther
(even) said on one occasion that 'for more than a week Christ
was wholly lost to me'. But his more characteristically defiant
attitude was this:

'And though they take our life,
    Goods, honour, children, wife,
Yet is there profit small;
    These things shall vanish all;
The city of God remaineth.'

In that assurance is peace. This peace is no false security; the
true Christian is not an escapist. He is a warrior, an apostle—if
need be, a martyr. But none may take his crown. John Kent's
testimony is that of the saints of the ages:

'What cheering words are these;
    Their sweetness who can tell?
In time and to eternal days,
    ''Tis with the righteous well'.'

* * * * *

A Hymn:

'Be still, my heart! These anxious cares
    To thee are burdens, thorns and snares,
They cast dishonour on the Lord
    And contradict His gracious word.

Brought safely by His hand thus far,
    Why wilt thou now give place to fear?
How canst thou want if He provide?
    Or lose thy way with such a guide?

When first, before His mercy-seat,
  Thou didst to Him thy all commit,
He gave thee warrant from that hour
  To trust His wisdom, love and power.

Did ever trouble yet befall
  And He refuse to hear thy call?
And has He not His promise passed,
  That thou shalt overcome at last?

He who has helped me hitherto
  Will help me all my journey through,
And give me daily cause to raise,
  New Ebenezers to His praise.

Though rough and thorny be the road,
  It leads thee home apace to God;
Then count thy present trials small,
  For heaven will make amends for all.'

(John Newton)

A Prayer:

'Grant unto us, Almighty God, the peace of God that passeth understanding, that we, amid the storms and troubles of this our life, may rest in Thee, knowing that all things are in Thee; not beneath Thy eye only, but under Thy care, governed by Thy will, guarded by Thy love, so that with a quiet heart we may see the storms of life, the cloud and the thick darkness, ever rejoicing to know that the darkness and the light are both alike to Thee. Guide, guard, and govern us even to the end, that none of us may fail to lay hold upon the immortal life; through Jesus Christ our Lord. Amen.'

(Rev. G. Dawson)

8

The Wondrous Plan

'What is the point?' A great deal depends upon the context
and the tone of voice in which that question is asked. It can be
asked in utter despair, and it sometimes is by those who feel
cheated by life and are contemplating suicide. It can be asked,
rather irritably, by a judge who is becoming increasingly
befuddled by the meandering testimony being presented to him.
Or it can be asked as I ask it here: in an eagerly questing way. I
want to know what is the point of the universe and of man. I
want to know what God's purpose is. I believe that there *is* a
purpose, and that 'the Lord's own plans shall stand for ever'
(Ps. 33: 11); but what are those plans? Paul took a lofty view of
God's purpose. It was, he said, 'that the universe, all in heaven
and on earth, might be brought into a unity in Christ' (Eph. 1:
10). This is a fine summary statement of the point I made
earlier, that creation and redemption are inextricably interwoven themes in Christian doctrine. The Fatherly God of
holy love created the world; he sustains it; he redeems it—and
all this for a purpose. All things are to be summed up in Christ.
That is one way of putting it, but there are other ways too—all
of them biblical.

We can speak of the consummation when God will be all in
all; we can speak of heaven as meaning eternal fellowship with
God; we can speak of eternal life as denoting a quality of life—
resurrection life—over which death has no dominion. But
perhaps the image which pervades the Bible more thoroughly
than any other is that of the Kingdom of God. In this final

chapter I shall look closely at this Kingdom and its King from the point of view of the plan of God; of God's ability to carry out his plan; and of God's motive throughout. As I go the cautionary voice of Elisha Coles comes to me across the years. Of God's sovereignty he said, 'This high and tremendous attribute, being an ocean that has neither bank nor bottom, may not lightly be launched into by any...without a divine compass, and an anchor within the veil.' My anchor is God's revelation in Christ, and my compass is the testimony of scripture and of Christian experience ancient and modern.

I

The Bible affirms God's sovereignty over all. He is King of the natural order: 'God is king of all the earth' (Ps. 47: 7). There is no rival to him, as Hezekiah's prayer reminds us: 'thou alone art God of all the kingdoms of the earth; thou hast made heaven and earth' (Isa. 37: 16; *cf.* I Chron. 29: 11). I dealt at length with this theme in my chapter on creation. In the chapter on God's providence I sought to show that the God who created all sustains all; and in the chapter on the problem of evil I showed how the sovereign Lord turns even the wrath of man to his praise. He brings good from evil. Nothing—not even a Cross—can thwart his loving purpose.

But there is an important distinction to be made. We might say that the natural order is under the sovereign hand of God 'without so much as a by your leave.' But man, God's free, responsible being, is able to spurn God's dominion, to rebel against his will, to close his heart against his love. And all of this is sin. Sin 'is self-coronation, wearing God's crown, carrying His sceptre, bearing His orb, mounting His throne. It is like banditry, it is spiritual piracy. It is the soul's proud boast: "We will not have Thee to reign over us"' (Vincent Taylor).

We have, then, two complementary ideas. First, God is sovereign over all—nature and man alike. But secondly, he is in a special sense the King of those in whose hearts he reigns. It is this latter idea which comes to the fore in the New Testament, and especially in the teaching of Jesus. Let us briefly trace the notion of God's sovereignty through the Bible.

In earliest times Israel thought that, like other gods, Jehovah had his own special people, and his own geographical territory. They came gradually to realise that there were no other gods (Isa. 46: 5), and that Jehovah's sway was universal. They came also to understand his rule in an increasingly ethical way. The great and mighty God, who indoubtedly makes covenant with his people, desires to write the terms of that covenant not merely on (external) tablets of stone as at Sinai, but actually on the hearts of his people (Jer. 31: 33).

By a sometimes painful process God's ancient people had to learn that Jehovah had not called them to be his favourites, but to be his agents in the world. They could not, therefore, claim immunity from judgement by incanting the correct phrases (Jer. 7: 4). On the contrary, from those to whom much had been given much would be expected (Amos 3: 2). Jehovah requires high ethical standards, worship from the heart, and an absence of hypocrisy (Hos. 6: 6; Mic. 6: 6-8, etc.)

Above all, Israel had to learn that God's sovereignty extended to all men. They could not with impunity adopt an exclusivist posture. If God desired to save heathen Nineveh, why should he not send protesting Jonah to that city? A comparatively few faithful ones continued to look forward to a time when God's universal sway would be acknowledged, though this hope became increasingly politicised during the years of oppression which preceded the Christian era. But when the Christ came, Simeon, in whose heart hope had never died, was in the minority (Lk. 2: 25). We thus have a history of God's gracious approach to his people. He made and renewed covenants with them; he sent them kings and prophets; but to a very large extent he met with rejection. The sovereign Lord was not honoured by his own. Likewise his Son 'entered his own realm, and his own would not receive him' (Jn. 1: 11). Small wonder that Christians looking back have ever seen the exilic prophet's Suffering Servant, who was 'despised and rejected of men; a man of sorrows and acquainted with grief' (Isa. 53), fulfilled in Jesus.

But the Christ did come! Had God been as humanly just as we sometimes expect him to be in the matter of punishing rebels,

he would never have sent his Son at all. He would have washed
his hands of us. But he is the *gracious* sovereign, whose holy
love tirelessly seeks and saves the lost. Still he comes, and in
Christ the promised Kingdom is inaugurated. Though yet to
come in all its fulness, it is here now. It is wherever God's kingly
reign is acknowledged. No longer are we thinking in terms of
territory. God's Kingdom has to do with relationships. It is in
the lives of those in whom he reigns as sovereign Lord.

II

The Kingdom of God (or of heaven) is not something which
men seek or 'bring in'; it is something which God gives. *He*
inaugurates his kingly rule in Christ. Under the preaching of the
gospel men are called into the Kingdom. Indeed the good news
is the good news of the Kingdom (Lk. 4: 43; 8: 1, etc.). To
preach Christ is to preach the Kingdom (Ac. 19: 8, etc.). The
Christ has come; the hour has come; the Kingdom has come—
these are all different ways of saying the same thing. And it is all
of God's doing.

Success is assured to the Kingdom of God. Its growth is
inevitable and irresistible, like that of the mustard seed which,
from a small beginning grows until birds (Gentiles) can nest in
its shade (Matt. 13: 31-32; Mk. 4: 30-32; Lk. 13: 18-19). Like
yeast which works its disturbing way in the dough, the Kingdom
is dynamic in the world (Matt. 13: 33; Lk. 13: 20-21). There are
wheat and tares in the field of the world (Matt. 13: 24-30); there
are good and bad fish in the sea (Matt. 13: 47-48); all will be
resolved in due course, and meanwhile the Kingdom makes
ground. Undeniably the seed of the gospel takes root in some
soils and not in others, but wherever good ground is found there
is a rich harvest (Matt. 13: 3-8; Mk. 4: 3-8; Lk. 8: 5-8).

The Kingdom is the Kingdom of the Fatherly God of holy
love. It is a Kingdom of grace. This is a most important point,
for everything turns upon the *kind* of sovereignty we envisage.
The Kingdom of God is the Kingdom of his Son. It is Christ's
no less than it is his Father's (Matt. 13: 41). The sovereign Lord
is the one we have learned to call Father through Christ—you

see why I began this book with God's revelation in Christ, and not with the abstract concept of sovereignty?

The sovereign God of Christianity is not the God of those Jews who looked for a show of military might to settle their grievances, and who therefore could not recognise Jesus as the Messiah when he came. He is not even the sovereign of John the Baptist whose latter day call to repentance, though in the tradition of the Old Testament prophets, demanded an obedience which *sinners* could not give. Christianity's sovereign is a Father whose heart bleeds for his lost children, and whose Son goes purposefully and willingly to the Cross for them so that by bearing their shame and vanquishing their sin he might call a new—and renewed—people to himself. God's purpose, said H. H. Farmer, 'is to fashion men through freedom into sonship to Himself and brotherhood to one another, or, more shortly, to build a kingdom of right and rich personal relationship, that is, of love—love being interpreted not in any sentimental sense, but in a sense as austere and demanding as the Cross'. Christianity's sovereign wins his way by humble service, by lowly love, by suffering. He lays down his life for his lost sheep (Jn. 10: 11). He rules graciously and without tyranny, placing his sons under the discipline of love (Matt. 11: 28-30; Jn. 14: 15; 15: 15).

Great harm has been done to theology and (more importantly) to tender consciences when the idea of sovereignty has not been adequately qualified by the ideas of Fatherhood and love. The truth is that we do not really have one idea qualifying another idea. What we have is the sovereignty of the Fatherly God of holy love who has made us *persons*. His nature is moral, his purpose is moral, and his methods are moral. He will not compel submission to his will; he does not coerce the mind, or violate the freedom he has given to us. He is no oriental despot. He is a Good Shepherd. His character determines his ways with men, as Richard Hooker realised long ago: 'The being of God is a kind of law to His working: for that perfection which God is, giveth perfection to that He doth.' God's sovereignty must be read through his revelation in Christ; and at the heart of that revelation is

'Sovereign *grace* o'er sin abounding'

(John Kent)

This grace is victorious, and because of it Josiah Conder bids the Christian be unafraid, for

'Your God is King, your Father reigns.'

The King is the Father; the sovereignty is paternal. That truth lies close to the heart of Christianity, and we know that it is so because of the Son who is Lord.

It comes as no surprise, then, to find that some of the best loved parables of the Kingdom tell of the Father's gracious, forgiving love to sinful men. There is the story of the labourers in the vineyard (Matt. 20: 1-15), which teaches that, contrary to the expectations of the 'religious', God treats alike all those who heed his call—whenever they heed it. This parable can provoke even a Christian's sense of injustice. After I had preached upon it a faithful worshipper said, 'But I have spent all my life in the Church; I began to teach in the Sunday School sixty years ago—surely God will take this into account over against those who make a death-bed repentance?' The parable proclaims that it is not so. We are not saved by works, but by grace; and that grace is God's free bestowal. Should we complain if he is generous? What a mercy that he does *not* treat us as we deserve! The owner of the vineyard *could* have paid one twelfth of the day's wage to those who had worked for one hour only; but he did not. As my revered teacher wrote, 'There is such a thing as a twelfth part of a denar. It was called a *pondion*. But there is no such thing as a twelfth part of the love of God' (T. W. Manson).

Again, there is the story of the Pharisee and the Publican, which tells of God's love for the repentant sinner (Lk. 18: 10-14). The publican, who confessed his sins, went home justified; the Pharisee, who thanked God that he was not like other men, did not. His self-righteousness shut him out from the love of God who delights to forgive sinners. Now this is by no means an easy parable to listen to—as the story of the Sunday School teacher shows. After recounting the parable to her class she said, 'Now children, let us thank God that we are not like the

Pharisee'—which is all very well until you realise that you are probably thinking, 'Thank God I'm not like the Sunday School teacher!'

But it is the fifteenth chapter of Luke's gospel which contains the cream of the parables concerning our Father-King's forgiving love. There we read of the lost sheep and the lost coin, and of heaven's joy when one lost soul is found. There too we read of the Prodigal Son. In the far country, having spent his inheritance, he came to his senses, prepared a speech, and set off for home. But his father, who had never cast him off, or ceased to love him, saw him in the distance and came running to meet him. He brought him in as a son, not a slave, and arranged a celebration meal. Such is the heavenly Father's love. But with the 'religious', sadly, it is often otherwise. They are represented by the elder brother, whose petulant reaction to the return not of 'my brother', but of 'this son of yours', shows that although he had never left his father's hearth he was miles removed from his heart.

These teachings of Jesus, and many more, make plain the kind of King with whom we have to do. But it would be a mistake to leave the matter there. We must go on to say that Jesus's whole life and ministry, and especially his death and resurrection, undergird the teaching and inform us of our King. Indeed, they do far more than inform—they *are* our King in action on behalf of sinners. For 'God was in Christ reconciling the world to himself' (II Cor. 5: 19). To be reconciled in Christ is to be in the Kingdom. No wonder Origen said that Christ is the Kingdom. And our reception into that Kingdom is all of grace. Philip Doddridge could hardly contain himself:

'Grace, 'tis a charming sound,
    Harmonious to my ear;
Heaven with the echo shall resound,
    And all the earth shall hear.'

III

I have just said that our reception into the Kingdom is all of grace; and so it is. But this statement needs to be elaborated.

God is sovereign over all; he is holy love. Man is free and a sinner. How can the sinner enter the Kingdom? There is a two-part answer to this question, and both parts of the answer must be held together. Men become members of the Kingdom both because they decide to, and because God calls them.

First, then, there is a decision to be made. We have to affirm who Jesus is, and commit ourselves unreservedly to him—as Peter did when at Caesarea Philippi, in answer to the question, 'Who do you say I am?' he blurted out, 'God's Messiah' (Lk. 9: 20). We have resolutely to declare, with the Church of the ages, 'Jesus Christ is Lord.' But even as we recognise who he is we see what we are. It is not at all surprising that the summons to repentance and faith stands at the beginning of the proclamation, and therefore at the gateway to the Kingdom (Mk. 1: 15; Lk. 7: 50, etc.).

The Kingdom is not something we slide casually into; it confronts us with a challenge. Are we willing to part with everything in order to possess it? Will we prize it above all else? Does a relationship with God matter *that* much to us? (Matt. 13: 44-46). Will the necessity of cross-bearing deflect us? Have we really counted the cost? (Lk. 14: 27-32). Are we prepared to leave all to follow Christ, or are we among those who make excuses? (Matt. 8: 19-22). As Matthew Henry wisely observed, 'There are many resolutions for religion, produced by some sudden pangs of conviction, and taken up without due consideration, that prove abortive, and come to nothing: soon ripe, soon rotten.' Or will we try to serve more than one master—God and money, for example? (Matt. 6: 24).

The decision to be made is not important for this life only. It has eternal implications. The End is coming; are we for Christ or against him? (Matt. 12: 30). There is no neutrality here. It matters which side we are on; and if we are for the Kingdom our lives must show it. The rich Jew, for all his impeccable religious pedigree, was being tormented. During his life he had daily passed by the needy beggar at his gate. He had not lived the Kingdom way. In the after-life the roles were reversed. Lazarus was happy, and the rich man called upon him for aid. (It was not that he had not noticed him by his gate—he even

called him by name!) To be of the Kingdom is to live under the
sway of, and in harmony with, the sovereign Father-God who is
holy love, and who challenges his sons to serve, and to love as
they have been loved: 'Anything you did for one of my brothers
here, however humble, you did for me . . . Anything you did not
do for one of these, however humble, you did not do for me . . .'
(Matt. 25: 40,45).

The salt must not become insipid (Lk. 14: 34-35); the light
must be seen (Mk. 4: 21); and since we do not know when the
judgement day will dawn (Ac. 1: 7) we must be on our mettle:
'Happy are those servants whom the master finds on the alert
when he comes' (Lk. 12: 37; *cf.* 39). Let us be warned by the
unpreparedness of the Foolish Virgins (Matt. 25: 1-13), and let
us be cautioned by William Gurnall: 'Christ hath told us He will
come, but not when, that we might never put off our clothes, or
put out the candle.' So much for the manward aspect of the
matter: our decision.

The God-ward aspect of things may be summed up in the
words 'election', 'calling'. Men are challenged to a decision
which is truly theirs, and for which they are responsible; but
God calls men, in grace and mercy, into the Kingdom. The
Father redeems men according to his eternal purpose (Eph. 3:
11), and during this life they are called into fellowship with him.

At once the thorny question is raised, 'What of those who are
not called?' Let us first have the humility to recognise that we
do not know who is not called. What we see are people who, so
far as we can tell, have not responded positively to God thus
far. The parables of judgement and warning make that a serious
enough condition to be in, but there is no New Testament
justification for the view that God from eternity predestined
some to damnation. It is true that in the course of his argument
in Romans ix-xi Paul considers the possibility of such a decree
of reprobation. But I believe that to Paul this was a theoretical
possibility only. If we read the chapters concerned as a unit, and
if we set them alongside all that Paul has to say elsewhere about
God's gracious, free, election, much of the difficulty is removed.
Paul is saying here that God *is* free to consign men hither and
thither; he has passed the Jews by because of their refusal of

Christ; but Paul goes on to say that God's goal is that Jew and Gentile alike will one day enjoy the blessings of the Kingdom together.

When views of a sovereignty insufficiently qualified by what we know of God's love in Christ have been held, we arrive at a God only minimally removed from the Stoics' necessitarian Fate. We find ourselves at a considerable distance from the God of whom it is said that he does not will that any should perish (II Pet. 3: 9). The Christian may and should rejoice in the words, 'You did not choose me: I chose you' (Jn. 15: 16); but he has no warrant for drawing conclusions concerning the eternal fate of those who do not at present believe. I repeat that this is in no way to exclude the possibility that some may be so persistent in their hostility to *holy* love that they are excluded from the Father's eternal family circle. We have no warrant at all for supposing that of necessity all will be saved:

> 'The lost are lost by refusing [the] gospel in their mysterious and incalculable freedom ... The self-determining power of the individual is part of the ordered predestination of God, and of the necessity felt by His love to endow man with a freedom like His own if He expected man to respond to His own. Only a fatalist predestination, not a personal, excludes such freedom.'
>
> (P. T. Forsyth)

To Joseph Alleine we owe one of the more refreshing of Puritan outbursts on this subject: 'Whatever God's purposes may be, I am sure His promises are true. Whatever the decrees of heaven may be, I am sure that if I repent and believe I shall be saved; and that if I do not repent, I shall be damned. Is not this plain ground for you; and will you yet run upon the rocks?' There you have the proper mixture of assurance and agnosticism, and the entire avoidance of speculation concerning others' eternal state. It is a cardinal principle of good theology that it should build upon what God has seen fit to make known to us, and not upon what he has not.

The experience of the Christian is that God has called him—not indeed because he was worthy of being called, but because God is gracious. This theme runs right back into the Old Testament where we read that it was not so much that Israel chose God, but that he chose them, and that not because of any special worth that Israel possessed, but rather the reverse: 'It was not because you were more numerous than any other nation that the Lord cared for you and chose you, for you were the smallest of all nations; it was because the Lord loved you and stood by his oath to your forefathers . . .' (Deut. 7: 7-8).

It is all of grace. This has been the testimony of believers in every age. The believer knows that he cannot barter or buy his way to God. He knows that

> 'Nothing in my hand I bring,
>   Simply to Thy cross I cling.'
>
> (A. M. Toplady)

Here the two aspects come together. Faced by the challenge of the Kingdom a man makes his choice. But as he enters the Kingdom—even more as he lives and grows in the Kingdom—he realises increasingly that the crucial thing was not his decision, but God's call to him in the gospel. He comes to see that even the faith which he reposes in God was first given to him by God. 'The idea of a human choice is the language of the newly converted . . . the certainty of the divine choice is the language of the sanctified' (N. H. Snaith):

> 'I sought the Lord and afterward I knew
>   He moved my soul to seek Him, seeking me;
> It was not I that found, O Saviour true;
>   No, I was found by Thee.'
>
> (*The Pilgrim Hymnal* 1904)

IV

So much for the nature of the Kingdom, the character of the King, and the way into the Kingdom. Underlying all that I have said has been the notion that the King is competent to bring his purposes to pass. In a word—the word I left over from chapter IV—he is omnipotent, *al*mighty. What God said of his old Israel may be said with even firmer conviction of his new:

> 'I have taken you up,
>   have fetched you from the ends of the earth,

and summoned you from its farthest corners,
    I have called you my servant,
have chosen you and not cast you off:
    fear nothing, for I am with you;
be not afraid, for I am your God.
    I strengthen you, I help you,
I support you with my victorious right hand.'

(Isa. 41: 9-10)

There could be no firmer guarantee of the triumph of the Kingdom.

But as with sovereignty, so with omnipotence: the word must be defined in relation to what we know of God in Christ. Out of our minds must go any idea of sheer force. The power of God is employed in a way which is thoroughly consistent with his character—otherwise it would not be the power of *God*. How many theological wrangles would have been avoided, and how much less ink spilled, if this had always been remembered!

On the one hand there have been those whose idea of God has been almost grotesque. They have represented him as being absolutely able to do absolutely anything. In one of his books Dr Sydney Cave reminds us of the Muslim tradition that when God created men from a lump of clay he broke it in two parts. He threw one part into hell saying, 'These to eternal fire, and I care not!' He threw the other part to heaven saying, 'These to Paradise, and I care not.' But Dr Cave goes on to point out that this capricious representation of God has appeared even in Christian theologies, especially when predestinarian theory has been divorced from what we know of God in Christ. Again, when Duns Scotus and William of Ockham defined God's will as 'absolute indifference'—by which they meant that God could literally, regardless of consistency, do anything that occurred to him—theology soon found itself in muddy waters. Ockham said that if God had so desired his Son could have become incarnate in a stone or an animal. The Church at large, however, has always insisted that what God does is consistent with his character as holy love. Christians do not know, worship and serve a God of sheer arbitrariness.

Aquinas argued that God could do everything that it is

intrinsically possible to do. This led to all kinds of speculations. Could God do what was logically impossible? Could he make a square circle? Or, as a child once asked, could God make a stone that was too heavy for him to lift? Whenever we move away from the God we know in Christ, and begin to propose abstract, theoretical tasks of this kind, our understanding of God's omnipotence is in danger of being trivialised if not completely distorted.

On the other hand some, like Schleiermacher, have taught that God can do only what he actually does. His omnipotence is limited by his performance. This, it seems to me, goes too far in the opposite direction—and how could Schleiermacher know that this was the case?

As so often, the middle course is best, and in this case it is biblical too. In our chapter on God's attributes we saw that the Christian God is no inconsistent, fluctuating deity. He is ever true to himself; in this sense he cannot change (Jas. 1: 17); nor can he lie—he is the God of truth (Num. 23: 19). Again, he cannot sin (Jas. 1: 13). Christopher Ness put it in a nutshell: 'All things (but lying, dying, and denying Himself) are possible to God.' And Stephen Charnock went to great lengths to explain that although God had the power to do many things which he did not will to do, his positive actions are always consistent with his perfections. I make his finding my own: 'The want of a right understanding of this doctrine of the divine power hath caused many to run into mighty absurdities; I have therefore taken the more pains to explain it.'

God's omnipotence, then, is not sheer, unconditioned might. Nor is it such as to violate the freedom he has given man. Despite man's often calamitous abuse of his freedom, God, as I showed in the last chapter, permits this abuse and redeems it. We may therefore conclude that his objective is a Kingdom of free and freed men, of men in harmony with himself. He will go to a Cross before he will remove that which makes man man. I like the way Dr Whitehouse puts the point:

> 'The measure of divine omnipotence, it has been said, is not the thunderbolt but the Cross. But notice that it is precisely in virtue of God's perfect power that He is able

to leave genuine room for human freedom. We know, from everyday experience, how freedom is imperilled by human tyranny, and the odd thing is that the men best able to let others act freely are themselves the greatest and most powerful . . . Paradoxical though it may seem, the Father's complete sovereignty and perfect power are the only sure ground of man's freedom.'

Our King is the King who is holy love; his omnipotence is the omnipotence of holy love. 'Love is omnipotent for ever because it is holy' (P. T. Forsyth).

V

Long ago God said to his ancient people, 'I will become your God and you shall become my people (Lev. 26: 12). It shall and must be so because of the one who said it. The sovereign Father desires fellowship with his people, and he will have it. Omnipotent holy love is more than competent to succeed. The end is assured. The Kingdom, here in embryo, will come in all its fulness. In this connection Jesus speaks of 'the coming of the Son of Man,' and of 'the Day'; and Paul looks for the time when God will be all in all (I Cor. 15: 28). In that Day

'All Thy works, O Lord, shall bless Thee;
    Thee shall all Thy saints adore:
King supreme shall they confess Thee,
    And proclaim Thy sovereign power.'

(Richard Mant)

The Christian is called to look forward in hope to that Day. Some find this a hard thing to do—and I speak here of believers, not of sceptics. It is hard when doubts, sufferings and difficulties assail. On such occasions we need the assurance that

'His purposes will ripen fast,
    Unfolding every hour;
The bud may have a bitter taste,
    But sweet will be the flower.'

(William Cowper)

Again, the thought of the coming Kingdom can be obliterated from our minds by the joys of this present life. At such times we need to remember that 'The comforts of this world are as candles that will end in a snuff, whereas the felicity that flows from an eternal God is like the sun, that shines more and more to a perfect day' (Stephen Charnock).

The Christian is a pilgrim, and he marches on until he reaches that city 'whose architect and builder is God' (Heb. 11: 10): that city, of which Augustine wrote, 'There we shall rest and see, we shall see and love, we shall love and we shall praise. Behold what shall be in the end without end! For what other thing is our end but to come to that Kingdom of which there is no end?' This is the Christian's goal—and God's; and as we go towards it we are sustained by hope: 'Hope can see heaven through the thickest clouds; hope can see light through darkness, life through death, smiles through frowns, and glory through misery. Hope holds life and soul together; it holds Christ and the soul together; it holds the soul and the promises together; it holds the soul and heaven together; and so it makes a Christian to stand and triumph over all afflictions, oppositions, and temptations' (Thomas Brooks).

Not indeed that the Christian is so intent upon the future that he overlooks the opportunities of the present. Although, because of the Cross-Resurrection victory, we know that the final victory is assured there is meanwhile work to be done. God has other sheep to call (Jn. 10: 16), and a task for his Church to perform (I Pet. 2: 9). Sons of the Kingdom are servants of the Lord and of their neighbours for his sake (I Pet. 1: 2; 2: 9). Citizens of the Kingdom are what they are by grace, and there is no privilege without responsibility. God has called and is calling his people, and by the quality of their lives they show their gratitude for his mercy. It has been well said that 'the way you argue about the ethical side of the covenant begins, "I beseech you, therefore, by the mercies of God..."' (J. Huxtable). The bearing of good fruit is the inevitable consequence of genuine surrender (Jn. 15: 8), and William Gurnall cautions us that 'Nothing more unbecomes a heavenly hope than an earthly heart.'

'The Kingdom of God,' wrote T. W. Manson, 'is, in the highest and purest sense, a paternal government. God is most truly King because he is most truly Father. And, on man's side, the yoke of the Kingdom becomes easy and its burden light, just in proportion as it is realised that it is the badge, not of servitude, but of service, and service of such a kind that the King who is our Father gives far more of it than he receives.'

One final word needs to be said in connection with the Christian's deportment in the Kingdom. It has been implicit throughout, but as a counter to unhealthy individualism I shall make it explicit. There is no Kingdom comprising one subject only. Life in the Kingdom is a life of fellowship with God and with other people. The good news of the Kingdom brings the Church into being (which is not to say that the visible Church is co-terminous with the Kingdom—remember the wheat and tares!). Not least among the challenges of the Kingdom is that of really caring for those in the next pew.

VI

I have spoken of God's purpose, and of his competence to achieve his end. But what is his *motive*? Jonathan Edwards was but one among many who have maintained that God's 'Last End in Creation' is his own glory. He reminds us that Jesus taught his disciples to pray 'Hallowed (or glorified) be thy name' (Matt. 6: 9; Lk. 11: 2); that Jesus regarded worthy living as a means of glorifying God (Jn. 15: 8); and above all that when Jesus was praying to his Father prior to facing the Cross his supreme objective was that his Father should be glorified (Jn. 17). Now as with sovereignty and omnipotence, so with glory: we must understand God's glory in relation to his character as revealed in Christ.

Thus, it is not the case that God needs our worship in order to be God, though as our Father he delights in it. Again he is not, as some have thought, being selfish in having his own glory as his supreme motive. For far above his delight in being glorified by his grateful sons is his desire to *manifest* his glory. That is, he desires to make himself known as he truly is: as the sovereign Fatherly God of holy love. How does he do this? In Christ. 'He came to dwell among us, and we saw his glory, such glory as befits the Father's only Son, full of grace and truth'

(Jn. 1: 14). The gracious God of creation, providence and redemption 'has caused his light to shine within us, to give the light of revelation—the revelation of the glory of God in the face of Jesus Christ' (II Cor. 4: 6). All of which brings us back to where this book started.

Hear the testimony of Hugh Ross Mackintosh, which I humbly endorse:

> 'In Christ we come in contact with the last and highest reality in the universe—our Father, perfect in love, in righteousness, in power. Taught by Him who has made the Father real, near and sure to our faith, we are persuaded that salvation begins with a Love which is eternal, and that in the realization of its designs there can be no breakdown. This is no conviction we should hide. Let it be told out rather with exhilaration, as one vital element in Christian gladness and security. Let it be laid down as the foundation of all our inextinguishable hopes for that Kingdom into which through His Church God is calling men—the Kingdom which is righteousness, and peace, and joy in the Holy Spirit.'

Of course there is much more to be said about who Christ is and what he does; about the work of God the Holy Spirit in taking of the things of Christ and showing them to us; about that fellowship into which we are called which knows no bounds of space or time; and about the climactic trinitarian confession to which those of the fellowship have been led. But the first thing was to begin with the God whom Christ makes known. A Christian doctrine of God cannot begin from any other point.

* * * * *

An Exhortation:

'Fear God for His power, trust Him for His wisdom, love Him for His goodness, praise Him for His greatness, believe Him for His faithfulness, and adore Him for His holiness.'

(John Mason)

A Hymn:

> 'How vast the treasure we possess!
>   How rich Thy bounty, King of grace!
> This world is ours, and worlds to come;
>   Earth is our lodge, and heaven our home.
>
> All things are ours; the gifts of God,
>   The purchase of a Saviour's blood;
> While the good Spirit shows us how
>   To use and to improve them too.
>
> If peace and plenty crown my days,
>   They help me, Lord, to speak Thy praise;
> If bread of sorrows be my food,
>   Those sorrows work my lasting good.
>
> I would not change my blest estate
>   For all the world calls good or great;
> And while my faith can keep her hold
>   I envy not the sinner's gold.
>
> Father, I wait Thy daily will;
>   Thou shalt divide my portion still;
> Grant me on earth what seems Thee best
>   Till death and heaven reveal the rest.'

(Isaac Watts)

A Prayer:

Thanks be to God for his creative power which gives us life;
Thanks be to God for his watchful providence which daily
sustains us;
Thanks be to God for his superabundant grace which
incorporates us into that Kingdom which has no end.

service; our lives radiate your love; and our hope be grounded
on your promise. These things we ask for your glory's sake.
AMEN.

Descriptive Index of Persons

(Biblical and fictional names are not included here)

Bushnell, Horace (1802–1876), American Congregational divine, 42

Calvin, John (1509–1564), French Reformer and theologian, 4, 9, 57, 81, 89, 103

Cave, Sydney (1883–1953), Congregational minister and theologian, 39, 132

Celsus, second-century pagan philosopher, 19

Chadwick, Samuel (1860–1932), Wesleyan minister, 77

Charnock, Stephen (1628–1680), divine, 8, 25, 39, 63, 66, 67, 69, 83, 133, 135

Chisholm, Thomas O. (1866–1960), American Methodist hymn writer, 30

Cicero, Marcus Tullius (106–43 B.C.), Roman Republican orator and philosopher, 6

Clarke, William Newton (1841–1912), American Baptist theologian, 65

Clement of Alexandria (c. 150–c. 215), theologian, 31

Coles, Elisha (1608?–1688), Puritan lay theologian, 122

Condor, Josiah (1789–1855), Congregationalist, editor, publisher and hymn writer, 15, 126

Cotterill, Thomas (1779–1823), Anglican hymnologist, 15

Cowper, William (1731–1800), poet and hymn writer, 117, 134

Crewdson, Jane (1809–1863), Quaker hymn writer, 100

Cudworth, Ralph (1617–1688), Cambridge Platonist, 109–110

Darwin, Charles (1809–1882), biologist and evolutionary theorist, 77, 109

Davidson, Andrew Bruce (1831–1902), Scottish minister and Old Testament scholar, 9

Davies, Samuel (1723–1761), American Presbyterian minister and hymn writer, 84

Dawson, George (1821–1876), Nonconformist preacher, lecturer and politician, 119

Deck, James George (1802–1884), Brethren hymn writer, 33

Denney, James (1856–1917), Scottish minister and theologian, 67

Dick, John (1764–1833), Scottish minister and theologian, 91

Dickie, John (1875–1942), Scottish minister and theologian, 14, 60

Dionysius the Pseudo-Areopagite (c 500), mystical theologian, 55

Doddridge, Philip (1702–1751), Nonconformist minister and hymn writer, 127

Downton, Henry (1818–1885), Anglican divine and hymn writer, 40

Dugmore, Ernest Edward (1843–1925), Anglican divine and hymn writer, 87

Duncan, John "Rabbi" (1796–1870), Scottish minister and Professor of Hebrew, 20, 73

Duns Scotus, Johannes (c. 1264–1308), Franciscan philosopher, 132

Edwards, David Miall (1873–1941), Congregational minister and theologian, 106

Edwards, Jonathan (1703–1758), American Calvinist philosopher and theologian, 83, 136

Epictetus (c. 55–c. 135), Stoic philosopher, 30

Erigena, John Scotus (c. 810–c. 877), philosopher and theologian, 112

Faber, Frederick William (1814–1863), Catholic priest and writer of hymns and devotional works, 26, 47

Fabre, Jean Henri Casimir (1823–1915), French entomologist, 86

Farmer, Herbert Henry (1892–   ), United Reformed Church minister and theologian, 84, 95, 125

Fawcett, John (1740–1817), Baptist minister, 102

Fisher, John (1459–1535), Bishop of Rochester, Cardinal, scholar and martyr, 46